THE US ARMY
★ IN WORLD WAR II ★

THE US ARMY
★ IN WORLD WAR II ★

MARK R. HENRY ★ ILLUSTRATED BY MIKE CHAPPELL

THE MILITARY BOOK CLUB #4

OSPREY MILITARY

First published in 2001 by Osprey Publishing,
Elms Court, Chapel Way, Botley, Oxford OX2 9LP, United Kingdom
Email: info@ospreypublishing.com

Also published an Men-at-Arms 342: *The US Army in World War II (1) Pacific*,
Men-at-Arms 347: *The US Army in World War II (2) Mediterranean* and
Men-at-Arms 350: *The US Army in World War II (3) North-West Europe.*

ISBN 1 84176 441 8

Editor: Martin Windrow
Design: Alan Hamp
Originated by Colourpath, London, UK
Printed in China through World Print Ltd

02 03 04   10 9 8 7 6 5 4 3 2

FOR A CATALOGUE OF ALL BOOKS PUBLISHED BY
OSPREY MILITARY AND AVIATION PLEASE CONTACT:
The Marketing Manager, Osprey Direct UK,
PO Box 140, Wellingborough,
Northants, NN8 4ZA, United Kingdom.
Email: **info@ospreydirect.co.uk**

The Marketing Manager, Osprey Direct USA,
c/o Motorbooks International, PO Box 1,
Osceola, WI 54020-0001, USA.
Email: **info@ospreydirectusa.com**

www.ospreypublishing.com

Dedication

To World War II veterans PFC John Holmes (65th Armd Inf/20th
Armored Division); PFC Richard Slaughter (39th Inf/9th Infantry Division);
Sgt Richard Rarick (504th Parachute Inf/82nd Airborne Division); Lt
Waldo Heinrichs (89th Infantry Division); T/Sgt Bill Mauldin, Willie & Joe;
and 'The Benevolent and Protective Brotherhood of Them What Has
Been Shot At'.

Acknowledgements

The author would like to recognise and thank the following
individuals and organisations for their assistance: Larry Corbett, Scott
and James Brustmaker, Robert & Alex Hargis, Frederick Spiller, Starr
Sinton, Bill Mauldin, Gil Whitley, Juan Gonzales (WW2 Impressions),
James and Carol Henry, Virginia Aparicio, Jonathan Fong, Martin
Windrow, Col Bob French (Ret), 1st Infantry Division Museum
(Cantigny), Grant Sigsworth, Karl George, Garry James, Cory Cline,
Ellen Guilmette and Frank Hanner of the US Army Infantry Museum
(Ft Benning). I would especially like to acknowledge and recommend
the books by Messrs Whiting, Gawne, Forty, Stanton, Canfield and
Perret in whose footsteps I follow. Unless otherwise noted, all photos
are from US Army/CMH or National Archives sources.

Editor's Note

The first section focuses on the Pacific Theatre of Operations. It
includes general information on infantry unit organisation; summer khaki
uniforms; officers' insignia; WAAC uniforms and insignia; service
medals; combat uniforms – HBTs, camouflage uniforms, the 'M1941'
Parsons jacket, helmets, footwear, and wet weather clothing; web combat equipment; small arms, grenades and flamethrowers; and rations.

The second section focuses on the Mediterranean Theatre of
Operations (North Africa, Sicily, the South of France and Italy). It covers
the organisation of Armored, Airborne, Mountain, Ranger, African- and
Japanese-American units; uniforms specific to the specialised units, as
well as cold weather clothing, and the M1943 combat uniform; NCOs'
insignia; gallantry decorations; crew-served weapons; and, briefly,
radios and transport vehicles.

The third section focuses on the North-West Europe campaign 1944-45.
It covers service dress uniforms and insignia, and includes notes on the
equipment of Armored, Mechanised Cavalry and Tank Destroyer units,
and tactical doctrine; the major artillery pieces, including anti-tank guns;
engineers; and replacement and demobilisation practice.

Each of the three sections includes a campaign summary, and a listing
of divisions that served in that theatre, with notes on their shoulder
patches. As detailed information on Airborne and Ranger unit history,
uniforms and insignia can be found in other Osprey books, little space
has been devoted to them in this title. The US Army Air Force is a distinct subject, covered in depth in the Osprey titles Elite 46 & 51. As
always in books from a British publisher dealing with an American subject, some inconsistency in style is inevitable. British spelling is
generally used but all US 'proper names' – unit titles, etc. – are given
in the correct US spellings.

Errata
In Plate E2 of the North-West Europe section, the M1 carbine is shown
with a bayonet lug. While these did appear before the end of the war
they are not known to have reached the ETO before the end of
hostilities.

CONTENTS

THE PACIFIC

Okinawa, 1945: a wounded GI is helped to the rear by a carbine-armed medic. Typically, they wear their HBT shirts tucked in and trouser cuffs loose; both types of the large-pocket HBT shirts are worn here. The medic's special pouches are pushed back to hang behind his hips on their yoke suspenders; his M4 bayonet is carried on a Japanese leather belt.

THE ALLIED WAR EFFORT in the Pacific may be divided into four theatres of operations: China-Burma-India (CBI), and the South, South-West and Central Pacific. Historians have generously highlighted the inter-service rivalries which these separate theatres – and the leading command personalities responsible for them – engendered. Books and movies have given prominence to the role of the US Marine Corps in its dramatic island battles in the Central Pacific. Virtually the entire burden of the ground war in the Burma/India theatre was borne by the British and Indian forces, and in China by the Chinese Nationalist army, although US air and logistic support was vital throughout the CBI. In New Guinea the Australians made a major contribution to the South-West Pacific campaign.

The British troops in Burma considered themselves a 'forgotten army', their long, costly, and eventually victorious campaign over-shadowed at home by the war against Germany; and over-arching all local rivalries is the odd fact that the US Army, too, seems to be barely remembered for its critical role in the Pacific theatre. The Army contributed more than 20 combat divisions to the ground war against Japan – three times the strength of the US Marine Corps; and it was the Army which stood the first shock of the enemy after Pearl Harbor.

* * *

The active strength of the US Army in 1939 was 174,000, making it a third-rate power. With war on the horizon, a peacetime draft – conscription, which filled local quotas by ballot – was instituted in 1940. It was renewed by Congress in 1941 by a margin of just one vote. The Army was dramatically enlarged, and by July 1941 it stood at more than 1,300,000, with 29 divisions and growing. By 1940 the Army was strong enough to hold its first corps-level manoeuvers since World War I. (A corps was a grouping of two to five divisions, and an army was a grouping of two to five corps.)

Army enlistment was filled by both volunteers and draftees. The rapidly expanding National Guard (Reservists) units were called to the colours and provided some 270,000 men to the Army. The draft included men from the ages of 21 to 35; the lower limit was later dropped to 18 years, but the average age of soldiers was 26, compared to 23 in the US Navy. High peacetime physical standards were steadily eroded to increase the intake, although about one-third of the draftees examined were rejected. Men were inducted for three-year terms, or the duration of hostilities plus six months.

African-Americans were accepted as both volunteers and draftees; they were formed into all-black units mostly officered by whites. A small number of combat units were formed, but generally blacks were posted to support units. Because of ETO manpower shortages in late 1944 they

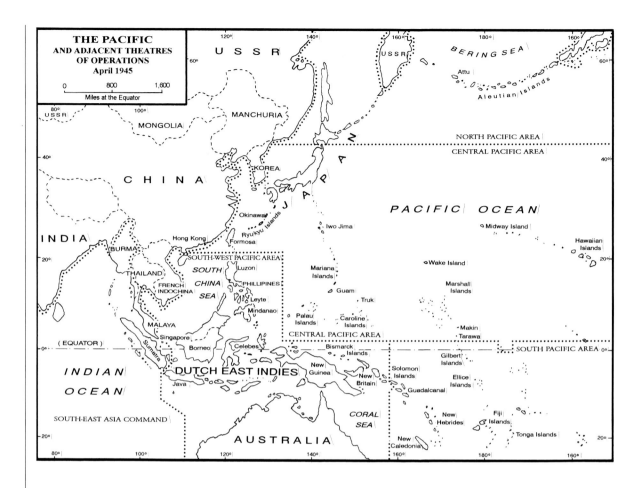

The Pacific and adjacent theatres of operations, April 1945.

were slowly integrated into white combat units as replacements. The 92nd and 93rd Divisions were all black, and by 1944 10% of the Army's manpower was black.

Beginning in 1942, women were accepted as volunteers in the Women's Army Auxiliary Corps (WAAC). In 1943 the WAAC was formally incorporated into the Army as the Women's Army Corps (WAC). By the end of the war about 100,000 WACs would be serving in the Army, including some 6,000 in the South-West Pacific and 10,000 in the European theatre.

New inductees were prodded, inoculated, and given intelligence tests to help the Army place them. The majority of the high test scorers were snapped up by the Air Corps or one of the technical support branches; some of these men were allowed to attend college and were to be inducted at a later date after acquiring important skills (the ASTP programme). Uncle Sam provided new recruits with a full 'government issue' (GI) of clothing, equipment and other necessities; and once caught up in the giant military machine they began to think of themselves as 'GIs', too. Basic training was cut to eight weeks after Pearl Harbor but later rose to a standard 17 weeks. These new men were used to fill out existing Regular, National Guard or new draftee divisions.

The senior officers of the Army were products of the new staff schools at Ft Benning and Leavenworth, and many were veterans of the Great War. Colleges (universities) provided a large cadre of junior officers to start with, but the Army would require many more leaders. With the US

Military Academy at West Point tardy in speeding up their four-year curriculum, Army Chief of Staff Gen George C.Marshal founded Officer Candidate Schools (OCS). These OCSs went on to successfully provide 65% of the officers required by the US Army. Promising enlisted men with four to six months' service could be recommended. At first they received 90 days of training in their branch and as leaders, and they soon acquired the nickname '90 day wonders'. The courses were later expanded to about 120 days, but the name stuck. Officers were also created by direct commissioning of civilians with special skills such as doctors, lawyers and engineers.

Ambitious Army planners envisioned that the US would need 200 divisions to achieve victory in Europe and the Pacific. In order to approach this goal it was found necessary to constantly comb men out of existing divisions to create cadres for new units; for instance, the 1st Division lost 80% of its strength in 18 months to these periodic drafts, and the 69th Division lost over 150% of its strength in the 16 months prior to its commitment to combat. This policy severely damaged the ability of existing divisions to train and build a team.

By 1945 8,300,000 men had been enrolled in the Army and Army Air Corps, with a stabilised combat strength of about 91 divisions.

ORGANISATION

In the late 1930s the Army began to reorganise its divisions. The old, musclebound 24,000-man 'square' division built around four infantry regiments was slimmed down to a 15,500-man 'triangular' division with three. With its new organisation and weapons the triangular division essentially retained its firepower but increased its flexibility and mobility. By 1943 the infantry division was further slimmed to 14,253 men, still organised around three infantry regiments.

In the Pacific the Army employed standard infantry divisions almost exclusively. Exceptions included the US/Filipino 'Philippine Division' of 10,000 men which was destroyed on Corregidor in 1942; and the 13,000-strong 'Hawaiian Division' of 1941-42, which was disbanded to provide cadres for the formation of the 24th and 25th Divisions.

The 11th Airborne (8,200 men) and the specially configured 1st Cavalry Division also served in the Pacific. The Army's horse cavalry consisted of two divisions in 1941. The 1st Cavalry Division (basically two rifle regiments and eventually four artillery battalions, totalling with support units about 12,700 men) was dismounted and served as infantry in New Guinea and the Philippines. The 2nd Cavalry Division was dismounted and converted into a black infantry formation, but was disbanded in 1943. The crack US/Philippines 26th Cavalry Regiment (Philippines Scouts) was destroyed in the fight for Bataan – the starving garrison ate their horses.

An important tactical innovation was the Regimental Combat Team (RCT). These were task forces temporarily extracted from divisions,

1942: Gunners strip to the waist to serve their 105mm howitzer. They wear HBT trousers without cargo pockets, and the man in the left foreground wears the first pattern HBT shirt with 'take-up straps' on the waistband. All wear the khaki first pattern floppy hat or 'Daisy Mae'.

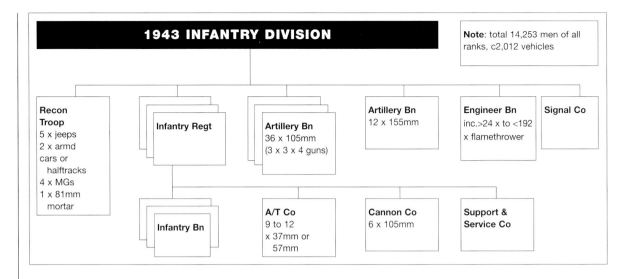

1943 INFANTRY DIVISION

Note: total 14,253 men of all ranks, c2,012 vehicles

Recon Troop
5 x jeeps
2 x armd cars or
  halftracks
4 x MGs
1 x 81mm mortar

Infantry Regt

Artillery Bn
36 x 105mm
(3 x 3 x 4 guns)

Artillery Bn
12 x 155mm

Engineer Bn
inc.>24 x to <192 x flamethrower

Signal Co

Infantry Bn

A/T Co
9 to 12
x 37mm or
57mm

Cannon Co
6 x 105mm

Support & Service Co

or independent units under corps control. Some RCTs and other independent units were combined on New Caledonia in 1942 to form the 23rd 'Americal' (America/Caledonia) Division. Most common among army/corps level independent combat units were mechanised cavalry groups and squadrons, and artillery, anti-aircraft, tank and tank destroyer battalions. These were attached to divisions or corps as required. Particularly in Europe, these attachments were common and almost permanent. If these combat units had been assembled into formations the US would have fielded approximately 15 additional divisions.

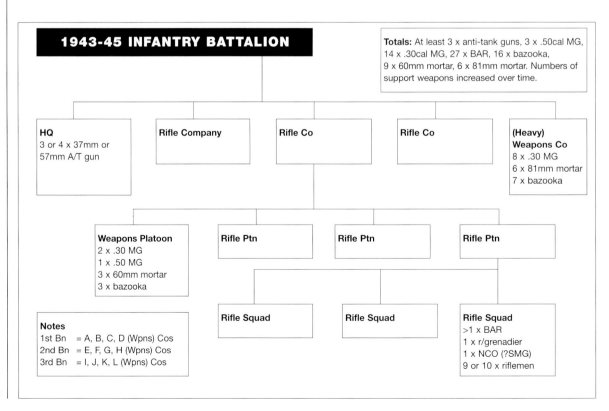

1943-45 INFANTRY BATTALION

Totals: At least 3 x anti-tank guns, 3 x .50cal MG, 14 x .30cal MG, 27 x BAR, 16 x bazooka, 9 x 60mm mortar, 6 x 81mm mortar. Numbers of support weapons increased over time.

HQ
3 or 4 x 37mm or 57mm A/T gun

Rifle Company

Rifle Co

Rifle Co

(Heavy) Weapons Co
8 x .30 MG
6 x 81mm mortar
7 x bazooka

Weapons Platoon
2 x .30 MG
1 x .50 MG
3 x 60mm mortar
3 x bazooka

Rifle Ptn

Rifle Ptn

Rifle Ptn

Rifle Squad

Rifle Squad

Rifle Squad
>1 x BAR
1 x r/grenadier
1 x NCO (?SMG)
9 or 10 x riflemen

Notes
1st Bn = A, B, C, D (Wpns) Cos
2nd Bn = E, F, G, H (Wpns) Cos
3rd Bn = I, J, K, L (Wpns) Cos

Infantry organisation

An infantry regiment (4,000 men) had a headquarters company, three infantry battalions, an anti-tank company (9 to 12 x 37mm or 57mm guns), a cannon company (6 x 105mm guns) and a support and services company. In the Pacific the regimental cannon company sometimes had light 75mm or 105mm pack howitzers. Battalions were commanded by majors or lieutenant-colonels and regiments by full colonels. The divisional artillery ('divarty') consisted of one 155mm battalion (12 guns) and three 105mm (36 guns). Regimental cannon companies were often absorbed into the divisional artillery. Later in the war self-propelled 105mm guns (M7 Priests) were substituted for the 105mm towed guns.

A 1943-45 infantry battalion consisted of 871 men in a headquarters, three rifle companies and a weapons company. Companies were 187 strong and consisted of three rifle platoons and a weapons platoon. A company was commanded by a captain, a rifle platoon by a lieutenant or sergeant. By 1943-44 a battalion (heavy) weapons company had eight machine guns, six 81mm mortars and seven bazookas. The rifle company's weapons platoon had two .30cal machine guns and one .50 cal, three 60mm mortars and three bazookas. Battalion HQ initially had three 37mm (later 57mm) anti-tank guns; by 1944 these were usually consolidated at divisional level.

At full strength, each of the platoon's three rifle squads consisted of 12 men and was led by an NCO. It was supposed to have ten riflemen, a rifle grenadier (armed with the 03 Springfield rifle), and a Browning Automatic Rifle man, providing the squad's light automatic support fire. Once in combat this configuration soon broke down, and GIs carried what was expedient and available. A squad might commonly add or substitute a 'tommy-gunner', a bazooka or an extra BAR man.

UNIFORMS

The Army started the war in khaki and brown drab uniforms and buff khaki (OD#9) webbing gear; by the end of the war olive drab (OD) green began to predominate. The term 'OD green' quickly came to mean any flat green colour from olive to dark green. The official shade (OD#7) was a darkish green characteristic of vehicles, 1943-45 combat clothing and web gear.

Khaki service dress ('chinos')

Khaki cotton shirts and trousers were standard Class C issue throughout the war for wear in summer and in hot climates ('khaki' is used throughout this text in its American meaning of a pale sand colour, equivalent to British 'khaki drill'). They were worn all year round in the South Pacific. The long-sleeved shirt had a six-button

A clear view of two garrison privates in khakis, c1941. Note the creased trousers, tucked-in ties, and campaign hats with coloured hat cords; enamelled metal unit crests were commonly worn on the front of these hats. They would soon be supplanted by khaki overseas caps. It was not uncommon, if somewhat provocative, for enlisted men to wear officers' quality items; the private on the right wears an officer's buckle.

In a training area at Hollandia in 1944 the 6th Army's Gen Walter Krueger (second right) discusses the merits of a Japanese 7.7mm machine gun with members of the 'Alamo Scouts' – a long range reconnaissance unit which he raised late in 1943, and which carried out its first mission in the Admiralties the following February. The group show a mixture of khaki shirts (with insignia), overseas caps and trousers, with green HBTs and fatigue caps; note the long bill of the ('swing' type?) cap at far right.

front and two breast pockets with clip-cornered straight flaps. Ties, when used, were black (M1936 and M1940) or more commonly khaki gaberdine/cotton (from 1942), and were worn tucked in below the second shirt button. Officers' shirts differed from the enlisted men's (EM's) version in having shoulder straps ('epaulettes'); an officer's khaki gaberdine shirt was also available as a private purchase. Some officers' shirts had square pocket flaps, some pointed or three-pointed. The matching trousers were straight cut, with slash side and rear hip pockets. An inch-wide khaki webbing belt with a bronze open-frame buckle was used with the EM's trousers; officers' belt buckles had a smooth brass face plate. Long khaki shorts were also authorised but rarely worn.

An officers' khaki cotton four-pocket service coat had been in use prior to Pearl Harbor. In September 1942 a khaki gaberdine version, with a slightly synthetic appearance, was authorised for officers; some early examples of this coat had a cloth belt. In the CBI, officers commonly wore variations on British khaki four-pocket tropical/bush jackets with US insignia added.

The visored khaki service hat (M1938) was standard issue before the war, but its issue was reduced in favour of the overseas cap (also commonly referred to as a garrison cap). This sidecap, inspired by British and French models, was first issued in the mid-1930s. It was later piped along the top and front edges of the turn-up curtain in branch of service colours (e.g. infantry, light blue); but by 1943 the EM's version was usually unpiped. Unit crests were sometimes pinned to the left front. Officers wore the same cap as the enlisted men but with mixed black and gold piping in place of branch colour, and with rank insignia pinned on the left front; general officers' caps were trimmed in gold.

In 1941, the Army's prewar Montana-peaked M1911 field/campaign hat also became a limited issue only, in favour of the overseas cap. A regimental crest was mounted on the centre front of the campaign hat; enlisted ranks wore branch-coloured hat cords, and officers mixed black and gold cords. This hat was sometimes worn with a narrow brown leather chinstrap.

Chinos were also intended as a combat uniform in hot climates but were rarely worn as such after the 1941-42 Philippines campaign. Khaki was rapidly found to be the wrong colour for battle, and the garments were entirely too lightly constructed. After the Philippines, it was agreed that the green herringbone twill work uniform was the only acceptable alternative for tropical combat.

Officers' rank insignia

Officers pinned their rank insignia near the end of coat epaulettes or on the right shirt collar. They were usually removed in combat to avoid drawing attention; indeed, in the Pacific the activities of enemy snipers made the wearing of any insignia on the battlefield quite uncommon. Officers sometimes pinned their rank under their collars or pocket flaps. (In combat in the European theatre an officer might wear his rank and

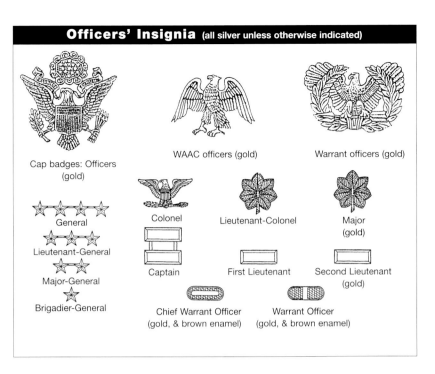

Officers' Insignia (all silver unless otherwise indicated)

Cap badges: Officers (gold)

WAAC officers (gold)

Warrant officers (gold)

General

Lieutenant-General

Major-General

Brigadier-General

Colonel

Lieutenant-Colonel

Major (gold)

Captain

First Lieutenant

Second Lieutenant (gold)

Chief Warrant Officer (gold, & brown enamel)

Warrant Officer (gold, & brown enamel)

branch insignia on his shirt collar under cover of a plain jacket.) Woven rank insignia in dull silver or golden thread were used as well as the metal equivalents.

Company grade officers were warrant officers, second-lieutenants, lieutenants and captains; field grades were majors, lieutenant-colonels and colonels; general officers were brigadier-generals and above. Warrant officers ranked below second-lieutenants but were officers and were saluted by enlisted ranks. The grade was created to fill special technical jobs; they had most of the privileges of officer rank with limited specific responsibilities. Warrant officers were commonly glider pilots, ordnance and administrative specialists, etc; they wore a special pattern of hat eagle badge and rounded bars for rank.

WAAC/WAC summer uniforms

The Women's Auxiliary Army Corps (WAAC) was created in 1942 to provide additional 'manpower' to the Army in administrative and support roles. They had only semi-official standing within the Army. The WAAC used Army rank insignia but had special rank titles, e.g. 'second officer' or 'third officer' and 'leader' for the equivalent of lieutenants and sergeants. They were paid at a rate one or two lower than their equivalent military rank. In 1943 the WAAC was converted into the Women's Army Corps (WAC) and became official members of the Army with full pay. In addition to 100,000 WACs, a further 60,000 members of the Army Nursing Service and some 1,000 WASPs (Women's Air Service Pilots) served in the Army in World War II; nurses and WASPs used their own uniforms and insignia, though their uniforms and the WACs' were eventually aligned.

Women (WAACs/WACs) initially wore khaki shirts and below-the-knee skirts for summer; for athletics and fatigue use in the USA they also had a light-coloured seersucker exercise suit to be worn with the 'Daisy Mae' hat. Officers additionally had a khaki cotton coat. The first model of this coat (initially with a cloth belt) had short transverse shoulder straps, false breast pockets, and slash pockets near the waist. The second model, available in 1943, had normal epaulettes; this was also authorised for enlisted wear in 1944. By 1945 a cotton khaki shirt and

A group of WACs in the USA, 1945. Except for the technical corporal (right), these women all wear either the one- or two-piece version of the women's HBTs in medium or dark green – note angled flaps on the thigh pockets – with the 'Daisy Mae' hat; . The 'tech corporal' wears the new 1945 khakis designed expressly for women, with an overseas cap bearing a unit crest.

trouser combination slowly became available. Except in extremely hot conditions, ties were always worn (tucked in). Brown laced low-heel shoes, an issue purse (handbag), and the infamous képi-style 'Hobby hat' in khaki were worn with this uniform. By 1944 a WAC pattern khaki overseas cap was available.

WAACs universally wore the helmeted head of Pallas Athena as the lapel insignia of their branch, and had a special plain eagle cap badge and button design. The later WACs wore either the Athena or the standard branch lapel insignia of their attachment, except in infantry and artillery assignments, when the Athena was worn exclusively. The WAC also replaced the rather sad-looking 'walking buzzard' cap badge of the WAAC with the standard US Army eagle.

Service medals

Several service or campaign medals were awarded to Army personnel in World War II. These were given as both the full medals (rarely worn) and as ribbon bars. Small metallic devices (appurtenances) were attached to the ribbons to show further service. Army ribbon bars were 1⅜in long and ⅜in high, and were worn in rows three or four wide. The mounting bars were originally pinback but by mid-war the modern style pin and clutch began to be used. Ribbon displays sewn on a cloth backing were also used by senior officers. Ribbons were authorised to be worn above the left pocket of service dress coats and sometimes of shirts, but not on combat or fatigue clothing. Gallantry awards were worn first (top), to be followed by (from the wearer's right to left) good conduct awards, campaign medals, and finally foreign awards.

The *American Defense Medal* was given to soldiers on active service between September 1939 and 7 December 1941; this medal distinguished the old regulars and National Guardsmen from the new draftees. A 'foreign service' slide was worn on the medal ribbon by soldiers serving overseas (including Hawaii and Alaska) between those dates; a small (³⁄₁₆in) bronze star on the ribbon bar represented this slide. This medal was authorised in late 1941.

The *American Campaign Medal* was awarded for one year's service in the Army between 7 December 1941 and 2 March 1946. Any combat service also qualified a GI to receive this medal. It was authorised in November 1942, and almost every soldier out of training would have received it.

The *Asiatic-Pacific Medal* ('A&P Medal') was authorised for service in that theatre between December 1941 and March 1946, and has precedence over the ETO Medal. A bronze star device was used to represent awards for participation in campaigns in theatre; a single silver star represented five campaign stars. There are 22 campaign stars possible in this theatre. An arrowhead device was used to mark participation in any amphibious or airborne operation; no more than one arrowhead was authorised for wear by any individual, but this rule was not always obeyed. The A&P Medal was authorised in late 1942.

The *European-African-Middle Eastern Medal* ('ETO Medal') was authorised for service in theatre between December 1941 and 8 November 1945; it was first issued in November 1942. Campaign stars and the invasion arrowhead were authorised as per the A&P Medal, and 16 campaign stars were possible for service in this theatre.

The *Good Conduct Medal* (GCM) was awarded to enlisted men who had completed a three-year enlistment with a clean record and superior efficiency. Only service after August 1940 counted. After Pearl Harbor the initial time period was reduced to one year. A tiny metal device shaped as a knot marked each additional award. Officers were not awarded the GCM, as they were always expected to display good conduct, though officers promoted from the enlisted ranks might wear it.

The *Purple Heart Medal* was awarded for wounds and some injuries received in action. (Frost-bitten feet qualified; trench foot did not.) Additional awards were represented by the use of oakleaf clusters on the ribbon.

The *WAC Medal* was awarded to Women's Army Auxiliary Corps members who agreed to enlist into the new WAC in 1943. Women joining the WAC after September 1943 were not eligible

The *World War II Victory Medal* was authorised for all members of the Army who had served between 7 December 1941 and VJ-Day, 2 September 1945.

COMBAT UNIFORMS

'HBTs and Frogskins'

New Guinea, 1942: a battalion commander from the 32nd Division with his staff. They all wear the first pattern HBTs with two-button waistband and pleated pockets (except the visiting Marine officer, who wears USMC pattern utilities with the classic breast pocket stencil). Some of the Army HBTs appear to have been dyed a darker black/green in Australia. The lieutenant-colonel carries a M1928 Thompson SMG.

The previous fatigue uniform of the Army was blue denim pants, shirt and 'Daisy Mae' – a floppy-brimmed hat nicknamed after a character in the popular hillbilly cartoon strip *L'il Abner*. In 1938 this was changed to medium weight sage green cotton cloth, woven in a herringbone twill (HBT) pattern. The blue denim remained the fatigue issue until 1941, however. The green of the original HBTs was found to fade quickly in use to an unsuitably light shade. In the Pacific this problem was sometimes remedied by vat-dyeing them en masse to a darker, even blackish colour. In 1943 the HBT manufacture colour was changed to the darker green OD#7 shade.

Most GIs felt that the HBTs were a bit hot and rather slow to dry, but generally pretty good. In North Africa and Europe HBTs were commonly worn as combat clothing alone or over brown woollen uniform for extra protection, camouflage and warmth. One 32nd Division Pacific veteran summed up the question of uniforms with the pithy and convincing comment, 'I don't believe there is any clothing or equipment adequate for jungle fighting'.

The HBT shirts all featured flapped breast pockets and exposed blackened steel '13 star' (or sometimes plain plastic) buttons. The M1942, the first of four patterns, had a two-button waistband with buttoning cuffs and rear 'take-up straps' (tightening tabs); the pleated breast pockets had clip-cornered flaps. The more common M1943 HBT shirt had larger breast pockets, but lost the buttoning cuffs and two-button waistband; it was made in a darker green than the first pattern. The first version of the M1943 shirt had unpleated pockets, while the next had a pinched sort of

Rendova Island, New Georgia, 1943: GIs wearing M1942 one-piece camouflage uniforms unload a Landing Craft Infantry (LCI). LCIs could carry 200 men; these shallow draft ships would drop anchor, then run aground on the beach, and after dropping their load they winched themselves off by the anchor chain.

pleat. The rarely seen last pattern HBT shirt (M1945?) was made with smaller pockets with clipped bottom corners and squared flaps. At the end of the war a new thinner cotton poplin fatigue was just beginning to be issued.

Rank was rarely displayed on fatigues, though NCO stripes were sometimes inked onto HBT sleeves. According to Capt Edmund G.Love, a 27th Division historian, this formation at one time had coded unit and rank symbols stencilled on the rear of the HBT combat uniform in black – a system copied from the US Marines. The division was identified by an outline parallelogram, enclosing unit symbols – e.g. a T, a 'bar sinister' and an Irish harp shape for the 105th, 106th and 165th Infantry Regiments respectively. Left of this, numbers indicated some ranks (e.g. 8 for sergeant, 15 for captain, etc), and right of it company letters were stencilled. Given the actual conditions of combat, and the frequency with which HBTs had to be replaced, it is doubtful if this complex system was maintained for long. Even in the six Marine divisions, which in 1943-45 seem to have had a thoroughly worked out system of back stencils, it is comparatively rare to see them in combat photographs.

Both HBTs and issue wool shirts commonly featured an extra length of material inside the buttoned closure, intended to be folded across to protect the skin against chemical agents; this 'gas flap' was sometimes cut out by the user. Trouser flys were also made with an extra interior flap of material for the same reason. (In the Normandy landings of 1944 chemically impregnated HBTs and woollens were worn by landing troops as a precaution against chemical warfare.)

The first pattern HBT trousers had sideseam and two rear pockets of a very civilian style. The second pattern (M1943) had thigh cargo pockets and sideseam pockets but no rear ones. The last pattern of the M1943 trousers had pleated thigh cargo pockets.

An HBT one-piece ('jumpsuit') work uniform had been designed in 1938 based on the B1 Air Corps mechanics' coveralls. In 1941, the M1938 was produced in HBT and featured a full buttoning front, an integral belt and a bi-swing/gusseted back; it had two each breast, rear and sideseam pockets. It was intended to be worn loose over other clothing, and the sideseam pockets opened to allow the wearer to reach inside. It was commonly worn by tank crewmen and mechanics but sometimes by other front line troops. It could be cumbersome to take off, and proved uncomfortably hot. A 1943 version was simplified and made in the darker OD colour.

In the field, women initially had to wear men's HBTs and woollens as little else was available. In 1943 one- and two-piece WAC HBT cotton fatigues became available. Both suits had angled flap front thigh patch pockets and used drab plastic buttons. The HBT shirt had two flapped patch pockets. Floppy 'Daisy Mae' hats were worn with HBTs, the special

WAAC issue having a slightly longer brim at front than back.

The first pattern (HBT) **camouflage suits** were issued in the South-West Pacific in 1943. This M1942 'frogskin' one-piece zippered suit had a green and brown coloured spot pattern on a pale neutral ground; the outside had a slight green cast to the pattern, and the lining camouflage a light brown cast. Despite this it was not truly reversible, having permanently sewn-in internal suspenders (though many GIs removed these) and pockets only on the outside surface. The suit had pairs of expanding breast and thigh pockets with two-snap flaps, and a gusseted back; the sleeves had a buttoned tab closure. The one-piece M1942 suit was too hot, and its design caused the users problems when responding to an urgent call of nature. The camouflage pattern was effective, but proved to stand out too much when the wearer moved. Some suits were later cut down into shirts worn with HBT pants.

By 1944 an improved two-piece HBT shirt and trouser suit was issued in the same camouflage pattern. It had the same pocket arrangement as the one-piece, although the buttons were concealed. This outfit – which was distinctly different in a number of details from equivalent garments produced for the US Marine Corps – proved more popular than the one-piece suit. Reconnaissance troops and snipers were heavy users of these 'frogskins', but green HBTs were still the most common GI combat clothing in the Pacific. (Camouflage uniforms were experimentally issued to some troops in Normandy in 1944, but were quickly withdrawn due to their dangerous superficial similarity to German Waffen-SS camouflage clothing.)

The 1940 'Daisy Mae' floppy hat was produced first in khaki, then in HBT green for field and motorpool use, and was sometimes worn into combat in the Pacific. In 1941 a short-billed HBT fatigue cap (M1941) was produced, reminiscent of a railroad engineer's cap. The 11th Airborne Division had its own modified khaki version of the M1941 (the 'swing hat') made with a longer bill. These two caps proved popular, and a longer-billed version was produced in 1944.

'M1941' field jacket

The short M1941 (PQD-20) or 'Parsons' jacket was designed in 1940 by Gen Parsons, and went into production later that year. (The term 'M1941' is widely used by today's collectors, but was not the contemporary designation; this was simply the 'Jacket, Field, Olive Drab'.) It featured a greenish khaki exterior and a flannel/wool lining, with a buttoned front fly over a zip fastener, an integral rear half-belt, buttoning tabs at the wrists and hips, and two diagonal front 'handwarmer' pockets with

TOP **Philippines, 1944: a team of 1st Cavalry Division long range scouts wear the one-piece 'frogskin' suit, and have painted their soft OD fatigue caps with camouflage colours. All are armed with M1 carbines, the rear centre man with a paratrooper's folding stock version.**

ABOVE **1944: both floppy hats and billed fatigue caps are worn here, with HBT cargo-pocket trousers, by a 4.2in mortar crew; the tube commander (right) still wears the one-piece HBT with 'bi-swing' back. The 4.2in (106mm) mortar excelled at putting down smoke/white phosphorus or HE; it became available in 1943, and units were normally corps-level assets assigned as needed.**

buttoned flaps. After several rapid modifications mass production began in 1941 and continued until late 1943. The full production version of the jacket had gussets behind the shoulders, and added epaulettes; the front pocket flaps of the first version were eliminated. It was manufactured in 12 sizes of windproof cotton 'Byrd' cloth or cotton poplin. This jacket was intended for light combat wear, and would be supplemented by the woollen overcoat or the raincoat in seriously bad weather. A thigh-length M1941 arctic or officer's coat similar to a mackinaw was also produced in limited numbers. A women's version of the Parsons jacket was made thigh length with reversed buttoning.

Infantrymen were too heavily burdened to carry overcoats and raincoats as a matter of course, so had to rely on the Parsons field jacket for most of their needs; and it quickly garnered a significant body of complaint. It was too short and lightly constructed to stand up to the weather. It showed dirt, and quickly took on a grubby appearance. The jacket's exterior faded to a light khaki drab that could stand out too visibly; on occasion GIs actually wore the jacket inside out to lessen its signature. Soldiers also sometimes removed the collar as too ill-fitting for comfort.

Despite the later issue of the improved M1943 combat jacket, the M1941 stayed in use throughout the war. In Europe, though never particularly popular, its continued wear became a trademark of an old soldier. It remained the most common jacket to be seen in the CBI and northern Pacific until VJ-Day.

Helmets

Initially, soldiers used the manganese steel US M1917A1 'dishpan' style helmet, with a rough sand surface and non-reflective OD finish. By mid-1942 large numbers of the M1 steel 'pot' were available. This helmet was to remain in US service until the mid-1980s. The chinstrap attachment brackets were fixed (welded) on the sides of the M1 helmet shell until 1945, when hinged brackets were introduced. Both helmets used a khaki canvas chinstrap with a claw-and-ball fastener.

The unusual feature of the M1 was its light fibre helmet liner which nested inside the steel shell and contained the webbing and leather suspension. The first model liner was thick-edged and made of compressed fibre covered with fabric; a thinner bonded cloth and plastic liner soon replaced this. Both types had a narrow brown leather chinstrap, normally worn up over the front brim of the steel shell. Liners were sometimes worn as separate headgear by GIs away from the front lines.

Florida, January 1943: these two sweater-wearing GIs are undergoing amphibious training. At right is the original Parsons jacket with pocket flaps, at left the more common flapless version. Both men wear M1 helmet liners without the steel shell, as was common in garrison and training.

Okinawa, 1945: lightly equipped GIs of the 96th 'Deadeye' Division look for a place to deploy their Browning M1919 air-cooled machine gun. All wear cargo-pocket HBT trousers and buckle boots. The two-month fight on this island would cost the 10th Army about 7,500 killed and 32,000 wounded.

On board ship en route for New Guinea, late 1942: GIs of the 32nd Division armed with a mix of Garands and Springfields – the latter probably for rifle grenadiers only. Note locally-made cloth helmet covers, and first pattern HBTs with buttoned cuffs. Their kit is stowed in general purpose barracks bags.

Some units in the Pacific and Mediterranean painted their helmets in camouflage patterns of large green and brown blotches or smudges. By 1943 helmet netting for the attachment of foliage was available; but as the Japanese used helmet nets, Pacific theatre GIs usually did not. Burlap covers were sometimes fashioned; and in the Pacific, US Marine Corps camouflage covers were also used occasionally. A cumbersome anti-mosquito helmet netting (face veil) cover was later issued. Helmet markings of rank and unit symbols were somewhat common in Europe, but almost unknown in the Pacific. The usual way of wearing a helmet in all theatres was without a net and with the canvas chinstrap pushed up over the rear brim, or left dangling.

The GIs found the M1 steel pot to be a versatile piece of gear; one Army nurse declared that it had 21 uses. Besides headgear, it was most commonly used as a washbasin, entrenching tool, or seat.

Another headgear used by the Army from 1941 was the sunhelmet. This was to be seen early in the war, and was made of a khaki-covered molded fibre; it had numerous grommet airholes and a narrow leather chinstrap. It was later reissued in a slightly darker greenish khaki. The sunhelmet was unpopular and rarely seen in use in the field.

Footwear

The red/brown 'russet' leather ankle boot (actually termed the 'service shoe') was used by the Army for both garrison and field use in 1941. Called by collectors 'type 1', it was made 'smooth side out' with a toecap and a leather sole. The 'type 2' model of the US ankle boot appeared in late 1941 and featured a composite rubber/leather sole. The 'type 3' boot of 1943 was a 'rough side out' version with an all-rubber sole. In mid-1943 a simplified 'reversed upper' ankle boot was issued; this was 'rough side out' and had no toecap. The 'type 3' and 'reversed upper' boots were for field use only and were heavily treated or dubbined for weatherproofing.

The M1943 or 'buckle boot' began to be seen in both the Pacific and ETO in late 1944 and rapidly became a favourite. It was made of rough-out leather, and its 16in (40.6cm) height, incorporating an ankle piece closed by straps and two dull steel buckles, obviated the need for leggings. It replaced both the ankle boot /leggings combination and the paratrooper boot as the standard Army-wide footwear.

The Army issued OD green socks of cotton and synthetic mix. These were usually made with extra material woven into the sole area for extra cushioning. Such socks are still issue in the current US Army. Off-white woollen winter or civilian socks were also used.

Light green/khaki M1938 canvas leggings were issued to be worn over the issue ankle boot, to keep out the dust, mud and bugs. Once they were in, the leggings kept them in – and also prevented water from draining away after wading. The standard pattern made of #6 duck canvas used nine brass hooks on the side for lacing, while later versions had eight hooks; each hook had two facing eyelets, so getting the leggings on or off was a time-consuming chore. In both the Pacific and Mediterranean theatres leggings were sometimes cut short or simply dispensed with. In hot weather trousers were commonly worn hanging unbloused over the leggings or boots.

In the Pacific, the coral sand and rocks and the sodden jungle floor abraded or rotted the soles off boots in a matter of weeks if not days. No real solution was found for this problem, though Australian-produced hobnailed GI boots provided better traction. (Hobnailed GI boots were also made in England in small numbers, and used in the ETO.)

Standardised in August 1942, a specially designed jungle boot began to be issued in the South-West Pacific late that year. It was essentially a canvas tennis shoe with the ankle extended to a height of 11ins (28cm). The sole, welt and toe were rubber, moulded directly to a green canvas upper and leg. Above the ankle the laces passed through hooks instead of grommets, for speed; and there was a full-length sewn-in bellows-type tongue behind the lacing. The jungle boot was light, dried quickly, and was good for quiet work; unfortunately it lacked support for the foot and ankle. The high top chafed the leg, and was often cut short. The jungle boots were only a limited success; but after the standard shoe they did not go unappreciated – one admiring Merrill's Marauder described the feel of them as like 'walking barefoot over the bosoms of maidens'. By 1945 a leather and canvas jungle boot not unlike the modern US pattern was developed, but it was too late to see wartime service.

Officers might wear any number of boots for field use, from the issue low-quarter to paratrooper boots. Special three-buckle, high-topped cavalry buckle boots were sometimes worn by senior officers.

Wet weather clothing
A rubberised drab canvas long raincoat (M1938) was standard. This unlined 'slicker' was liked in Europe but was too awkward and heavy to carry around all the time (and unfortunately, it also gave GIs

Leyte, 1944: this kneeling rifleman from a 96th Division machine gun team provides a classic view of the GI in the Pacific theatre. Note his smudge-camouflaged helmet, jungle first aid kit, two canteens, and M1936 musette bag worn as a pack (with a weapons cleaning kit protruding).

the same silhouette as greatcoat-wearing Germans). This raincoat had a five-button front and a broad vented back panel.

The Marine issue camouflage poncho was quickly copied by the Army in green for Pacific use. It served GIs as a tent section, groundsheet, equipment cover, and rainwear. It was issued first in a heavy treated canvas (weighing 3.2lbs – 1.4kg) and later in a form of straight green ripstop nylon (weighing 1.2 lbs – 0.5kg). It had a drawstring neck but no hood; the edges could be snap-fastened together to make sleeves.

WEB GEAR AND EQUIPMENT

The GI used 'improved M1910' webbing accoutrements throughout the war, these incorporating various improvements made since that date. Early war webbing was khaki to light green in colour, and much of it still bore World War I manufacture dates. As the war went on webbing gear was produced in a steadily darker OD green. Though metal snaps (press studs) were used on webbing items the most common fasteners were the so-called 'lift-the-dot' (hereafter, LTD) closures; these featured a sprung collar engaging with the neck of a raised stud, and functioned better when cold, muddy fingers were fumbling to open or close pouches. Webbing field gear was usually ink-stamped 'US'; it was produced by numerous manufacturers, and their stamped company names and dates were usually to be found inside a pocket or on the back. Various items like canteens, bayonets and aid pouches were hung by hooks from the many black metal eyelets along the edge of the webbing belts. By 1944 the QM started chemically treating all canvas gear to slow the rotting process common in the Pacific.

The basis of the rifleman's harness throughout World War II was the M1910/23/36 series cartridge belt; this had two five-pocket sections, each pocket holding two five-round steel stripper clips for the 03 rifle or an eight-round clip for the M1 Garand. Limited numbers of the M1938 12-pocket belt were also issued. Cavalry pattern M1910 cartridge belts were also used, and can be identified by a missing pouch on the left front. Additional expendable six-pocket cloth bandoleers (holding 60 rounds or six Garand clips) were issued to riflemen as they went forward into the line; a knot was tied in the cloth strap to adjust it.

The plain webbing M1912/36 pistol belt was intended for GIs who had no need to carry a rifle cartridge belt. Like the latter, the pistol belt had numerous metal eyelets for mounting associated web equipment as well as the M1928 backpack.

For the Thompson sub-machine gun a rarely-seen haversack-style pouch and strap were developed to hold a single drum magazine. A five-pocket pouch set with LTD fasteners was quickly issued for use with the 20-round box magazine, to be worn on the pistol belt. A three-pocket (LTD) pouch was available very late in the war for the 30-round magazines of the Thompson and M3 'greasegun'. A narrow haversack-type pouch for 30-round magazines was also available in the ETO.

Corregidor, February 1945: the airborne landing by the 503rd PIR was supported by an RCT from the 24th Division landed from the sea. The island was garrisoned by some 5,000 Japanese, mostly ensconced in massive tunnels; this 24th Division .30cal machine gun team watch over a damaged tunnel exit (the majority of the Japanese accidentally blew themselves up in two attempts to sortie out). Note, right, the characteristic method of carrying the basic first aid pouch hooked below the bigger jungle kit.

The M1937 Browning Automatic Rifle (BAR) belt had six BAR pockets each holding two 20-round magazines. Older belts of World War I manufacture were used early in the war, and many were retro-modified by the addition of a sixth pocket and the now standard smaller 3in bronze/steel belt buckle. A three-pocket bandoleer-style BAR pouch set was also made.

The M1936 web suspenders could be worn with any of the web belts to help distribute the weight of the belt order, but were initially issued only to officers for use with their M1936 'musette' bag. Simplified M1944 suspenders were issued late in the war. The notorious M1910/28 haversack (backpack) was overly complex when fully loaded, and an 'awkward carry'; being supported by suspenders rather than complete shoulder straps, it could only be worn in conjunction with the cartridge/pistol belt. In the assault it was packed much lighter and smaller. Unfortunately, to get something out of the pack it had to be laid out and fully opened. A blanket was carried by GIs rolled in a canvas shelter-half either in the lower pack section, or more commonly fastened horseshoe-style around the outside. As generally disliked as it was, the M1928 stayed in regular service throughout the war.

The M1943 jungle pack was the first issue replacement for the old M1928; essentially a long bag, it had integral shoulderstraps that allowed it to be worn without hooking it to a belt. It was made in both green canvas and camouflage pattern. GIs liked it, but it was never put into full mass production. The shortcomings of the M1928 were finally addressed in the M1944/1945 field packs. These very similar designs had two components – an upper field pack and suspenders, with straps for the attachment of a lower cargo valise, which could be left behind when going into combat. Made of dark green canvas, the M1944/1945 packs saw only limited issue before VJ-Day.

The M1936 field or 'musette' bag was normally used as a haversack (as was the M1943 gasmask bag). Officially an officer's item, it was also commonly used as a backpack by connecting the two carrying strap hooks to the D-rings on the front of the M1936 suspenders.

The canvas shelter-half was usually carried wrapped around a blanket horseshoe or folded within the pack. As with most 'pup' tents, this canvas sheet buttoned together with a partner's half to form a low two-man tent. Four wooden tent pegs, rope and a wooden tent pole were included in the set. Ponchos could also be snapped together to form a shelter. In the Pacific, a well-liked hammock was issued in 1944; unfortunately, GIs in the front line obviously could not expose themselves above ground to use it – and it proved to have a limited lifespan of only about 45 days, due to rot.

The long M1905/1942 bayonets were carried on the left side of the pack or belt; the common 10in (25.4cm) M1 bayonet was usually carried on the belt in a scabbard of laminated green plastic. The old M1910 'T-handle' or the M1943 'E-tool'

Ulithi Island, Carolines, 1944: an officer and men from the 81st Division disembark. The carbine-armed officer carries an entrenching tool, a long M1 bayonet, two canteens, a large jungle aid pouch and a first aid bandage pouch hooked to his rifle cartridge belt, supported by M1936 suspenders, and a slung haversack. The radioman has an SCR 300; and note the two nozzles of the inflatable lifebelt worn by the right hand man. Issued in 1943, the jungle first aid kit consisted of a field dressing, insect repellent, iodine, petrolatum (burn ointment), a tourniquet and some bandaids.

(entrenching tool) had canvas covers which could be hooked to the belt or the back of the pack. The M1908/1938 wirecutters were carried on the belt in a LTD open-top pouch.

A large multi-purpose haversack-style canvas ammunition bag was produced in 1943; this could hold a metal ammunition can (e.g. 250 rounds for the .30cal machine gun), multiple grenades or rifle grenades. In 1944 special three- and two-pocket grenade pouches were issued, each pocket holding two grenades. These unpopular items hooked to hang below the web belt, with tie-down leg tapes.

Medical orderlies wore a set of large pouches (M1942) to hold their supplies; they could be attached to the pistol belt as a pair, and came with special shoulder yoke suspension webbing. Some medics preferred to use plain haversacks or musettes instead.

All GIs carried a field bandage in a M1910/1942 pouch (LTD)on the front of the waist belt; a single-snap (non-LTD) version of the M1942 pouch was also made in England. The dressing was contained in a brass, canvas or plastic case. In the Pacific a more extensive 'jungle' first aid kit came in a larger, two-snap flapped pouch usually worn on the back of the belt.

The issue stainless steel M1910 canteen was based on the World War I aluminium version and held one quart; the World War I type had an aluminium cap, the M1942 version a black plastic cap. The one-pint canteen cup was carried in the bottom of the insulated canteen carrier, the canteen nesting into the cup and carrier. Early in the war some canteens were also made with a black or dark blue enamelled finish. In the Pacific it was not uncommon for GIs to carry two canteens into action. The company and year of manufacture is usually marked on both the canteen and cup. Small air bladders and later specially made bladder canteens were uncommon but popular in the Pacific for holding potable water. Water purification tablets and chlorine were sometimes carried.

Messkits based on the World War I pattern were used by all GIs for hot chow in the field. The two plate sides and the utensils could be hooked together and dipped into hot water for cleaning; the plates were made to clip together so that both could be balanced in one hand. In combat the most common mess items carried were canteen cups and spoons only. A small, simple hinged can opener usually came in the ration packs but was sometimes kept on a GI's 'dogtag' cord.

Soldiers initially used the voluminous green cotton barracks bag to carry the rest of their clothing and gear; this was soon replaced by the long strapped canvas dufflebag. Normally stamped with the owner's name, this was left behind when a soldier deployed to the front. A smaller waterproof tie-top bag was also issued to protect packed items (a similar bag is still on issue to this day).

Rations

The GI's food came up to the front lines as B-, C-, D- and K-ration packs. If the soldiers were lucky their food would be prepared by company cooks and brought up in thermal marmite cans. Small squad stoves, 'canned heat' or C2 explosives could also be used to warm rations. Toiletries, tobacco and candy were usually issued free to GIs in the divisional area.

The B-rations were group canned meals in large quantities – 5-in-1, later 10-in-1 (i.e. five meals for one man or one meal for five men). They were popular with the GIs, but too bulky to carry in combat unless you had a vehicle.

The D-ration was a 4oz chocolate and wafer bar, commonly included in the other ration packs. It could withstand temperatures of 120°F without melting, and was originally designed as an emergency ration. It was intended to taste bad to prevent it being eaten casually; this concept was soon reversed, though to little discernible effect. One veteran described it as 'very difficult to eat, hard as a rock, and rather bitter... I would shave it into small fragments to prevent tooth fracture'. It was nicknamed 'Hitler's Secret Weapon' due to its effect on some GIs' bowels.

The C-ration was originally limited to a range of only three canned meals: stew, hash, and pork and beans. In addition it usually included a D-bar, crackers, hard candy, dextrose (energy) pills, and coffee, cocoa and lemonade mixes. GIs found the very acidic lemonade powder mix to work excellently for scrubbing floors, but rarely took it internally. The C-ration pack was heavy (5lbs – 2.26kg) and bulky. Its contents were intended to be eaten only for a day or so, but front line GIs often had to eat them for weeks at a time, and rapidly grew to hate them.

By mid-1943 an accessory/condiment can of cigarettes, gum, toilet paper and water purification tablets (halazone) were added. A spaghetti meal was also added in 1943, and the range was extended until ten meals existed by mid-1944, with hash being dropped; and caramels were substituted for the dextrose pills. The C-rations were especially hated by Pacific GIs who had been dealing with them since 1942; the up-dated C eventually won acceptance, if no admirers. A soldier of the 37th Division said of the Cs, 'We hated them until we ran out and started to starve. Then the hash, wiener and beans, beef stew with a biscuit and condiment cans became winners'.

The K-ration became available in 1943 and was designed (initially, for paratroops) as an individual combat ration that was easy to carry and consume; two Ks could be carried for every C. They came in breakfast (veal), dinner (spam), and supper (sausage) meals, with condiments, cheese and crackers, candy and gum, drink mixes, toilet paper and smokes. The waxed ration boxes would burn just long enough to heat coffee water; they were originally issued in plain buff with black lettering but were later printed with colour-coded patterns. One veteran's summation was that '... usually the K variety was favoured over the C, but both were rather unappetising after weeks of the same'. (Units in Europe temporarily assigned to the British sector received English 'Compo' rations, much to their dismay.)

In the Pacific special jungle rations were tried out in 1942-43. They included spam, dried fruits/peanuts, crackers, cigarettes and gum. This

This GI photographed in the USA in 1942 seems less than enthusiastic about his canned rations and chocolate D-bar. He wears the prewar blue denim fatigues under his early-pattern Parsons jacket; his wool overseas cap is piped infantry light blue and bears the enamelled regimental crest of the 29th Infantry.

Philippines, 1944: an 81mm mortarman from the 31st Division gets a compass bearing as his tube is prepared for firing; like most machine gun and mortar crews he has a holstered pistol for self defence. Jungle packs and a machete are also evident. Broken down for carrying, this mortar's three components weigh about 44lb (20kg) apiece.

ration required too much water, and was too bulky, though GIs appreciated the fruit. In intense combat GIs usually ate only the candy and gum and dropped the rest. The Pacific theatre assault (candy) ration addressed this fact with 28 pieces of assorted hard candy, gum, cigarettes and a chocolate peanut bar. It was first issued in February 1944 and remained popular. Rice was also issued to GIs in the South-West Pacific.

Canned composite/luncheon meat – or as it was universally known to GIs, 'spam' – was a component of most of the rations, and they tired of it quickly. The main advantage of this meat was that it kept without refrigeration. It was provided to Britain and Russia in huge quantities during the war; Kruschev later declared that this 'Roosevelt sausage' sustained the Red Army. Unlike some other foods in the wartime USA it was never rationed.

SMALL ARMS

M1903 and M1 rifles

The .30 calibre M1903 Springfield was the Army's commonly available rifle in 1941. This five-shot rifle was based on the German Mauser bolt action system, and was known for its accuracy and reliability. The rifle was issued in a grey/green parkerised gunmetal finish. It weighed 8lbs (3.6kg), and was called a 'Springfield' or '03' by the GIs. 'For firepower or close range we'd use the M1 rifle or carbine, but for long range accuracy you couldn't beat the 1903 Springfield', remembered an ETO veteran of the 83rd Division.

A limited number of M1917 'Enfield/Eddystone' rifles were also used early in the war, especially in the Philippines. In 1942 the manufacture of the Springfield M1903A3 began. The most obvious difference was the movement of the modified rear sight from the front of the action to the back. Both the 03 and 03A3 remained in production by Remington and Smith-Corona until 1944, and the 03 was retained for launching grenades throughout most of the war.

The most commonly used sling for the 03 and the later M1 Garand was the M1907, made of russet brown leather with brass/steel claw adjusters. A simple khaki canvas web sling first appeared in 1943 and steadily became more common. Also to be seen in limited numbers were the khaki canvas M1917/ 1923 Kerr slings.

The 03 and M1 Garand also initially shared the 16in (40.6cm) parkerised blade M1905/1942 bayonet; the 10in (25.4cm) M1 bayonet began manufacture in 1943 and quickly became the norm. Many M1942 bayonets were arsenal-recut to 10ins (M1905E1). The M7 green plastic scabbard was worn on the side of the pack or on the belt.

The M1 Garand was the replacement for the 03 Springfield and is now recognised as the finest military rifle available at the time – Gen George S.Patton called it 'the greatest battle implement ever devised'. Approved for purchase in 1938, significant numbers were not to be seen until 1942, though a handful of M1s were used in the defence of Bataan. The Garand, produced by Springfield and Winchester, took the same bayonet and cartridge as the 03 but fired semi-automatically – eight rounds, as fast as the shooter could pull the trigger. It was 36ins (91.4cm) long and weighed 10lbs (4.5kg). The eight-round *en bloc* clip was loaded into the action from the top – rounds and clip together (and, if you were careless, your thumb too – 'M1 thumb' was a common malady). When the last round was fired the empty cartridge case and the steel clip were ejected together, the clip making a distinctive 'pling'.

The Marines had examined the M1, but decided in favour of retaining the 03; they also experimented with the Johnson semi-automatic rifle – a satisfactory design, but too fragile. As US industry was pouring out the M1, the Corps changed its mind and went with the Army's choice. On Guadalcanal many 03-armed Marines 'picked up' the prized M1 from reinforcing Army troops. By 1945 over five million Garands had been produced, and the weapon remained in limited production until 1957.

Snipers used the M1903A4 (Remington) with a Weaver 330C/M73B1 2.5 x scope and pistol grip stock. Surprisingly, this 03 was not specially accurised for sniper use, and the scope was found to be somewhat fragile for the battlefield. A sniper version of the Garand (M1C), including a laced-on leather cheekpiece and a scope, only became available late in the Pacific war.

The issued .30cal ammunition was the M2 ball cartridge; commonly referred to as '30-06', this had a copper-jacketed, sharp-pointed 'spitzer' bullet of 150 grains. This powerful, flat-shooting cartridge was issued in ball, armour-piercing and tracer variants. The propellant produced an unfortunately large muzzle flash and smoke signature when compared to Japanese and German ammunition.

Guadalcanal, 1943: this Garand-armed rifleman is commonly identified as a Marine, but his shirt with pleated pockets is first pattern Army HBT, and his ID tags are of the oblong Army shape rather than the much rounder USMC pattern. M1 Garands were also standard issue to the Army but not to the Marines at this date. Note also the thick, pale brim of his early issue helmet liner.

M1911A1 pistol

A slightly improved version of the Colt M1911 of World War I, this stalwart semi-automatic weapon was carried in action by officers, senior NCOs and machine gunners, among others. Made of parkerised steel, and holding seven man-stopping .45cal rounds, the much-loved '45' was in US service for more than 80 years. This pistol was carried in a 'US'-stamped brown leather flap holster (M1916) on the right hip; a two-magazine web pouch was mounted on the front of the pistol belt. A shoulder holster (M3/M7) was sometimes used by tank crews, officers and others. A drab lanyard was available but rarely used. (General officers were issued a special Colt pocket automatic in .32 or .380 automatic calibre.)

Revolvers

The .38cal Military & Police (M&P) Model 10 revolver was produced by Smith & Wesson; a similar pistol made by Colt was called the Victory model. Revolvers were issued to aviators and, in limited numbers, to MPs and others (it is a tradition to this day that aviators carry revolvers and not automatics). Front line troops rarely used this weapon. Some old M1917 .45cal revolvers were also issued in small numbers. Revolvers were carried in a brown leather M1909/17 or M2/M4 half-flap holster.

M1 carbine

Becoming available in 1943, this handy weapon was issued as a supplement or replacement for the .45 pistol, intended for officers and second line troops such as drivers, artillerymen, MPs, etc. The M1 carbine – sometimes called the 'baby Garand' – was made by ten different manufacturers, including IBM and Underwood Typewriters. It had a 15-round detachable magazine, and its weight loaded was a light 6lbs (2.7kg). Compared to the Garand's 30-06 round, the carbine used an anaemic .30cal cartridge that was little more than a souped-up pistol round; it was nicknamed 'the peashooter', and its lack of stopping power was always of concern. GIs liked the carbine for its light weight and its 15-round capacity, which gave it significant firepower; it rapidly became a common front line infantry weapon, being carried by many soldiers instead of the Garand. Riflemen were about evenly divided as to whether they preferred the Garand or the carbine; their opinions presumably depended on whether or not they had personally found themselves endangered by its lack of range and punch.

Bougainville, 1943: two GIs operating a jeep evacuation service for casualties. The 'hood ornament', wearing cut-off camouflage shorts and a billed soft cap, is armed with the M1 carbine; the driver wears a helmet liner. The jeep has been modified to take stretcher cases and, as was common in the jungle, has tyre chains fitted for traction.

M3 trench knives were usually issued to GIs who carried carbines; in late 1944 the M4 bayonet, based on the M3 knife, became available. This had a leather grip, and was carried in the M8 plastic scabbard. The carbine was not modified with an add-on bayonet lug (T4) until after the war. The folding-stock M1A1 became available in 1943 and was used primarily by paratroops. A two-magazine pouch designed to be worn on a pistol belt was also unofficially mounted on the buttstock of the carbine. The fully automatic M2 version of the carbine slowly became available in 1945, with a 30-round 'banana' magazine. The experimental T3 version, mounting an infra-red scope, was used at night in the last weeks before VJ-Day.

Sub-machine guns

Produced in 1919 as a 'trench sweeper', the blow-back operated Thompson sub-machine gun remained unwanted by the US Army until 1939. The fin-barrelled M1928 version of the .45cal 'Tommy-gun' was a complex and powerful machine pistol. Its identifying features were a top-mounted cocking handle, a 50-round drum magazine, and a slotted Cutts compensator on the muzzle to help control its tendency to climb during firing. The austere wartime M1/M1A1 versions had a side-mounted cocking handle, no barrel cooling fins, no compensator, and a simplified bolt. All variants took 20- or 30-round box magazines, but only the M1928 could use the 50- or 100-round drums. The Thompson's (M3) khaki canvas sling was a modified Kerr rifle sling.

The Thompson was well liked not only by GIs but by the British and Australians to whom it was also supplied in large quantities. It was commonly carried by squad leaders and junior officers. Its drawbacks were the high cost of manufacture; its short accurate range – about 50 yards; and a taxing loaded weight of about 14lbs (6.3kg). It fired between 600 and 700 rounds per minute, but feeding problems developed if it was not kept scrupulously clean. Its rate of fire and short-range stopping power were both appreciated; but in the jungle its report sounded dangerously like that of a Japanese light machine gun.

The 1943 M3 sub-machine gun or 'greasegun' was a simplified weapon made from easily stamped metal parts, and cost Uncle Sam $20 apiece. The M3 featured a handleless bolt that was charged by means of a thumbhole. It took the same .45 cartridge as the Thompson, but a different 30-round box magazine. It was commonly issued to AFV crews and was sometimes carried by infantrymen. It fired slower (400rpm) and, with its more crudely industrial appearance, was perceived – unjustly – as less reliable than a Thompson. The slightly improved M3A1 came out in 1945. Ugly, but light (8lbs – 3.6kg) and reliable, it was not universally admired but it had its faithful adherents.

Saipan, 1944: GIs from an engineering outfit search a dead Japanese. The M1 'tommy-gunner' with the 30-round magazine wears first pattern HBTs; the other two still have one-piece HBT suits. The kneeling man has his 'dogtags' taped together to keep them quiet; and a rarely seen 'CIO' brassard (Counter Intelligence Officer?)

Browning Automatic Rifle (BAR)

The M1918 BAR reached the trenches in 1918; it weighed 16lbs (7.25kg) and could be fired semi- or fully automatic, using the standard US 30-06 rifle cartridge. It was designed to be fired from the hip while moving rapidly forward in direct support of attacking riflemen. By World War II the modified BAR could be fired fully automatic only, at a slow 400 rpm or a fast 600rpm setting. With a bipod, hinged buttplate and carrying handle (M1918A2) it weighed over 20lbs; in the field it was commonly stripped down to its basic 16 pounds. As the rifle squad's main support weapon it tended to be used both as an automatic rifle and a light machine gun. In the former role it was an excellent and popular weapon; its shortcomings in the latter were that its barrel could not be field-changed when it overheated, and the 20-round magazine was a limitation on its firepower. A slightly shorter and lighter M1922 'Cavalry' BAR was also used in limited numbers.

M97/M1912 shotgun

Rarely available, these military 12 gauge pump-action 'riot' shotguns had their uses; they had limited range, but excelled in close combat, and were also used by MPs guarding prisoners of war. Limited numbers were definitely used in Pacific combat – Gen Patch was seen to carry one on Guadalcanal – although Gen MacArthur attempted to restrict their use. Ultimately, six different models of shotguns were accepted by the Army. The more common Winchester M97 and M1912 had a 20in (50.8cm) barrel, weighed about 8lbs (3.6kg) and carried six 00 buckshot shells in the tubular magazine under the barrel. The cardboard shells sometimes

THE PHILIPPINES, 1942
1: Corporal, US Infantry, Philippines Division
2: 1st Lieutenant, US Cavalry
3: Filipino rifleman

A

CALIFORNIA & HAWAII, 1942-43
1: Infantry private, guard duty, 1942
2: Captain, Women's Army Auxiliary Corps, 1943
3: Captain, Field Artillery, 1943

B

GUADALCANAL, 1942-43
1: Infantry private, 23rd Infantry Division
2: Rifle grenadier, 25th Infantry Division
3: Infantry sergeant, 23rd Infantry Division

C

SOUTH-WEST PACIFIC, 1943-44
1: Corporal machine gunner
2: Private second gunner
3: Private ammunition bearer

D

CHOWTIME, 1943-44
1: Sniper of an infantry unit
2: Medical orderly, 93rd Infantry Division
3: Staff sergeant of a Tank Battalion

PHILIPPINES, 1944-45
1: Officer, Ranger or Scout unit
2: Battalion commander, 11th Airborne Division
3: Private, 26th QM War Dog Platoon

F

OKINAWA, 1945
1: BAR gunner, 77th Infantry Division
2: Flamethrower operator, 77th Infantry Division
3: Infantry private, US Marine Corps

MISCELLANEOUS
1: Rifleman, Kiska Task Force; Aleutians, summer 1943
2: Supply sergeant, SW Pacific, 1943
3: 1st Sergeant, HQ US 8th Army; Japan, 1945

3a

1

3

2

H

swelled in the damp climate; full brass casings had solved the same feeding problem in France in 1918, and these were once again tardily made available in 1945.

Knives

Old knuckle-guard trench knives from World War I, USMC K-bars, individually ground-down bayonets and civilian hunting knives were all seen in use throughout the war. Issue of the newly designed M3 fighting knife began in late 1942. The M3 trench knife had a 7in (17.8cm) parkerised blade; its most distinctive feature was its bent thumb rest on the guard. A well-liked general purpose knife, it was issued in a metal-reinforced leather (M6) or later plastic composite (M8) scabbard. The similar M1 carbine bayonet (M4) was produced in 1944 and replaced the M3. (In Europe the 1st Special Service Force also had their own custom-made V42 combat knives.)

The M1939 machete had a 22in (55.9cm) blade made by Collins and came in a leather sheath; the M1942 had an 18in blade and a canvas or plastic sheath. The short, broad-bladed, pointed M1910/1917 and USMC Bolos were also used in limited numbers.

Makin Island, November 1943: a 27th Division BAR man awaits the enemy behind a fallen palm trunk. Note the front-to-back depth of the M1928 pack; and the large six-pocket BAR belt – each magazine held 20 rounds and each pouch two magazines, giving a basic load of 240 rounds.

Bougainville, 1944: a 37th Division GI winds up for the pitch, throwing his grenade baseball style – though most soldiers found the text book straight-armed lob to be the best method for throwing. Under magnification this GI can be seen to have his ID tags fixed together with a dark rubber rim.

Grenades

The MkIIA1 fragmentation grenade or 'pineapple' was based on the classic British No.18/No.36 series ('Mills bombs') used in both World Wars, though with a different design of igniter set and fly-off safety 'spoon'; it weighed 21oz (595g) and had a four-second fuse. Early-manufacture fuses emitted a loud 'pop' accompanied by smoke and sparks, and in the humid Pacific there were frequent 'duds' due to ignition problems; later improved fuses were more reliable. For the first year of the war the grenade came with the body painted entirely yellow (blue for training grenades). Later, just a yellow stripe around the top, or lettering, were the usual indicators of a filled grenade. Unlike the adequate German or weak Japanese types, US frag grenades were both powerful and deadly.

The 14oz (396g) MkIIIA1 model was a smooth-skinned HE/concussion grenade; GIs felt it to be dangerous to the user and less effective than the 'pineapple'. (Most armies of the day differentiated between high-fragmentation 'defensive' grenades, to be thrown at an attacking enemy from behind cover; and low-fragmentation 'offensive' grenades, to be thrown ahead of the advancing troops for concussion effect without endangering the thrower. The distinction proved to be more theoretical than practical.)

Smoke was commonly used to provide cover or to signal. The M16 cylindrical smoke grenades

(1943) were available in green, violet, orange, black, yellow, and red colours; the more effective M18 smoke came out in 1944. M8 (white) and M2 (red) smoke were also issued in limited numbers. These 'smoke cans' were painted blue-grey with a waist band and lettering in yellow, and the tops painted in the relevant smoke colour.

The M15 white phosporous (WP) grenade was excellent for smoke, starting fires, marking targets, and suppressing enemy bunkers. The heavy 31oz (878g) WP or 'Willy-Peter' was cylindrical, but had a semi-rounded bottom so as to be distinguishable from smoke cans by feel. It had a four-second delay fuse and a bursting radius almost wider than it could be thrown. The can was painted blue-grey and marked with a waist band and 'SMOKE WP' in yellow.

The M14 thermite grenade was used for signalling and for destroying machinery. This 32oz (907g) grenade had a two-second fuse; the blue-grey can was marked with a waist band and 'TH INCENDIARY' in purple.

Chemical (gas) grenades were rarely used in World War II, though M6 and M7 CN/DM teargas grenades were sometimes used to root out the occupants of bunkers and caves. Gas grenades were blue-grey cylindrical cans, marked with a waist band and 'GAS IRRITANT' in red.

Rifle grenades

Rifle grenades available to the GI came in anti-tank, smoke and parachute flare variants; they had a range of under 200 yards. A special unbulleted blank round was used to propel them, and a small M7 'vitamin pill' could be inserted to boost the range by 40-50 yards. The 03/M1917, M1 rifle and M1 carbine all used similar clamp-on muzzle devices. The M1/M1A1 grenade adapter was a solid, finned tube with a three- or four-pronged clamp which would hold a 'pineapple' (or even a 60mm mortar bomb). The 03 used the M1 launcher, which allowed the rifle to fire ball rounds while it was in place. The M1917 took the M2 launcher. The M7 grenade launcher for the M1 Garand began issue in mid-1944 but was unpopular since it did not allow ball rounds to be fired; the M7A2 did, but only became available after VJ-Day. In early 1944 the M8 grenade launcher attachment was added to the M1 carbine.

Most rifle grenades were fired at a high angle with the butt braced against the ground and turned sideways; M9/M9A1 anti-tank (shaped charge) grenades used contact fuses and were commonly fired from the shoulder at AFVs and bunkers. Both the 03 and M1 could use a rarely-seen rubber boot which covered the butt and absorbed much of the recoil. The wooden rifle stock could sometimes be damaged when firing grenades, the M1 carbine being particularly prone to a cracked stock; the use of the folding stock carbine as a platform was not recommended. Both

New Georgia, 1943: a rifle grenadier from the 27th Division helps a comrade down the muddy trail. The tommy-gunner (note 50-round drum) wears the one-piece camouflage suit; the taller GI has a rubber shock-absorbing boot on the butt of his M1903 Springfield. Strangely, the tommy-gunner wears a rifleman's cartridge belt and the other GI carries a large gasmask bag.

the soft ground and the corrosive climate of the Pacific made rifle grenades somewhat less popular there; they were also dangerous to use in thickly wooded terrain, with the risk of striking a treetrunk and bouncing back at the user.

Flamethrowers

The US Army of 1939 had no flamethrowers, but they were quickly developed by the Chemical Corps and issued to the combat engineers. The first model (E1-R1) came into use in 1942 in New Guinea but proved very weak and unreliable: '... Cpl Tirrell crawled through the underbrush to a spot some 30 feet from a Japanese emplacement. He stepped into the open and fired his flamethrower. The flaming oil dribbled 15 feet or so, setting the grass on fire. Again and again Tirrell tried to reach the bunker, but the flame would not carry. Finally a Japanese bullet glanced off his helmet, knocking him unconscious.' Poor design, fragility of fittings and the heat and humidity of the Pacific were hard on the E1-R1 and M1 models. The use of gasoline also caused projection problems. Dogged attempts to improve it paid off in the steadily more reliable M1A1 (1943) and M2 (1944) models.

In 1942 just 24 flamethrowers were assigned to a division; by 1944 they had become a key weapon in the Pacific, and the divisional scale of issue had reached 192. The successful M1A1 and M2 used one cylinder of propellant nitrogen and two cylinders of 'napalm' – jellied gasoline, with an improved range of 40-50 yards. The M1 and M1A1 flamethrowers weighed about 70lbs (31.7kg), and their 5gal fuel capacity gave all models only eight to ten seconds of fire. An assistant accompanied the flamethrower operator to turn on the tanks from the rear just before use; by 1944 the assistant was to carry a jerrycan of additional fuel. The E1, M1 and M1A1 had electrical spark ignition problems, so some teams carried WP/thermite grenades to insure that the target 'cooked off'. The M2 had a range of 50 yards and an improved pyro ignition system based on a Japanese method. Stuart and Sherman flamethrower tanks were also to be seen in the Pacific in 1944-45. (Flamethrowers were available in Europe, but not used in such numbers.)

Lone flamethrowers deployed without protection were usually suppressed or destroyed with little impact. By 1944 many Army (and Marine) divisions were organising specially equipped bunker-busting teams of

Okinawa, 1945: an M4 Sherman flame-tank ('Zippo') of the 713th Tank Bn hoses down a cave entrance in support of the 7th Division's advance. Shermans modified to take flamethrowers became available in mid-1944 and were heavily used on Okinawa; they could shoot flame up to 65 yards and sustain fire for about one minute. Although flame-tanks in the Pacific were quite widely dispersed in small numbers, the 713th was the only complete battalion.

15-25 men who used 'corkscrew and blowtorch' tactics. These teams were formed around two flamethrowers and included riflemen, BARs, demolitions men and bazookas. They used flamethrowers to burn off jungle cover to expose Japanese-held caves and log bunkers. Then riflemen, BARs and bazookas laid down suppressive fire as the flamethrowers approached. Flame shot across the gun slits forced the enemy back as the demolition teams closed; then combinations of thrown demolition charges, bazooka fire and close-range flame finished the job. Near the front lines, jeep-mounted refill/repair positions supported the still short-winded and fragile flamethrowers. These integrated teams proved highly successful, but not all divisions organised them.

Bougainville, 1944: a 37th Division flamethrower man checks out a burned Japanese bunker. By 1944 the improved M1A1 and M2 flamethrowers had become a integral part of small unit tactics for neutralising Japanese positions – the so-called 'corkscrew and blowtorch' method. Operators sometimes 'hosed down' targets to soak them with fuel before lighting them up.

Loading an amtrac; the LVT-4 of 1944 could hold about 34 passengers, and had a rear ramp, which made loading and unloading much easier and safer. Note the gull-winged track pattern. These men all carry the M1936 musette as a pack.

AMPHIBIOUS VEHICLES

In the Pacific, Mediterranean and North-West European theatres successful amphibious operations would prove critical to winning the war. Fortunately, in the 1930s the US Marine Corps – with very limited assistance from the Navy and Army – pursued doctrine and hardware to make these operations possible. A waterborne assault is among the most difficult manoeuvres an army can attempt. The costly failure of the British/Canadian 'raid in force' at Dieppe in 1942 foreshadowed disaster for any opposed amphibious landing. By 1943 the US was able to prove their amphibious equipment and doctrine to be sound and viable, and in the last two years of the war American strength and expertise in this challenging form of warfare became unsurpassable.

The standard landing craft of the war was the 'Higgins boat', designed by that company at the behest of the Marine Corps (over the objections of the US Navy). The Higgins boat or LCVP (Landing Craft Vehicle/Personnel) in all its variants was said by Eisenhower to have been one of the three tools that won the war for the Allies (the others being the C-47 Dakota transport aircraft, and the jeep). This floating shoebox with a front ramp carried approximately 36 combat-loaded soldiers. More than 22,000 LCVPs were produced before VJ-Day.

Primary among the Army's amphibians was the six-wheeled DUKW (universally known as the 'duck', although the title code letters officially stood for '1942 – amphibious – all wheel drive – dual rear axle'). Essentially an amphibious 2½-ton truck with a rudder and propeller for

water travel, it could simply drive down into the water and then drive out again on the other side. Developed in 1940-41, it came into Army service in 1942. The DUKW could travel at 45mph on land and 6 knots in the water, carrying 25 men or 2.5 tons of supplies. It gained early fame for an incident off Cape Cod in 1942 when an '... Army truck rescues men from a stranded naval vessel'. The Allies rapidly became dependent on the logistical link it provided between ship and shore. In the Pacific, the Army operated several amphibious brigades of DUKWs; US Navy-crewed DUKWs also supported landings in the Mediterranean and Normandy.

The Army also used the USMC-developed amphibious tractors or 'amtracs' to support their operations in the Pacific. This vehicle had been initially designed by John Roebling for civilian use as a 'swamp buggy'. The open-topped Landing Vehicle Tracked (LVT-1) or 'Alligator' was a fully-tracked amphibian that could cross reefs and sandbars to deliver troops on to the beach, propelled by its flanged track plates. With a crew of three, it carried 20-plus soldiers or 2 tons of cargo, and travelled at 25mph/4 knots; at least three machine guns could be mounted, but it was initially unarmoured, and was a transport rather than a fighting vehicle. The improved LVT-2 or 'Water Buffalo' which reached combat units in 1943 carried 24 men or 3 tons of cargo. Infantry had to clamber over the hull sides to disembark from the LVT-1 and -2; the LVT-4 (1944) and LVT-3 (1945) had rear ramps, and could carry a jeep and a 37mm gun, a 105mm gun, 4 tons of cargo, or at least 32 infantry.

The 'amtracs' soon gave birth to 'amtanks', armed and lightly armoured variants to provide fire support at the point of landing (though their inherent vulnerability was always recognised, and every effort was made to get 'real' tanks ashore as early as possible). The LVT(A)-1 and -2 of 1944 mounted the 37mm gun turret from the Stuart M5Al light tank; the LVT(A)-4 had an open-topped turret with a short 75mm howitzer. Small numbers of amtracs were also modified to carry flamethrowers, rocket projectors, several .50cal machine guns and 37mm aircraft cannon. The armour on the LVT(A)s was only capable of turning small arms fire, but their presence on the beach gave troops a critical firepower edge during the first minutes of a landing.

The USMC enjoyed priority of issue, and the first US Army amtrac battalions did not see combat until the Kwajalein landing in the Marshall Islands in February 1944; each had 119 LVTs organised in two 51-vehicle companies and a headquarters. In time the Army would actually outstrip the Marines in these units – 23 Army to 11 Marine amtrac, and seven Army to three Marine amtank battalions. By June 1944 in the Marianas the first Army amtank unit, the 708th Amphibian Tank Bn – which won a Distinguished Unit Citation on Saipan – had four companies each with 13 x LVT(A)-1s and 4 x (A)-4s, supporting the amtracs of the 534th, 715th and 773rd Amphibian Tractor Battalions.

Okinawa, 1 April 1945: over the top – GIs of the 96th Division clamber between the .50cals at the front of an amtrac and up a seawall at Hagushi beach. The 'April Fools Day' landing by four divisions was unopposed. These men wear the old M1928 packs; and note, centre foreground, a camouflage-painted helmet.

New Guinea, April 1944: M4A1 Shermans and infantry prepare for an assault up Pancake Hill, Hollandia. The GIs have fully loaded camouflage jungle packs; the tank crews wear both leather tanker and M1 steel helmets. At night the tanks would 'laager up' side by side, facing in opposite directions, to fend off any surprise attack.

TANKS IN THE PACIFIC

The only US Army tanks available in the Pacific at the time of Pearl Harbor were about a hundred M3 Stuart light tanks of the Provisional Tank Group (192nd and 194th Tank Bns), on Luzon in the Philippines. Although the M3 was under-gunned and under-armoured by international standards, the unit fought bravely and effectively against the even weaker Japanese Type 95s before the fall of Bataan.

By 1943 the heavier M4 Sherman began to become available, but until 1945 the improved M5A1 Stuart still equipped some companies of mixed tank battalions. The units in theatre represented about one-third of the US Army's total of tank battalions; none were organic to Army divisions in the Pacific – all were independent, assigned by corps or army as needed.

For the first half of the war the jungles and islands did not provide much of a field of use for the tank; and throughout the war its main role was in direct support of infantry, where its cannon and machine guns were of huge value in suppressing enemy fire and 'bunker busting'. Stuarts were fitted with flamethrowers in 1943; and the flamethrower-equipped Shermans of the complete 713th Tank Bn were particularly valuable in 1945 on Okinawa, where the bloody fighting sometimes resembled World War I trench warfare. Apart from the fighting on Luzon in December 1944-February 1945 tank-vs-tank actions were rare, and the US equipment was always superior to the Japanese. (On Peleliu in September 1944 US Marine Sherman crews used HE rounds to ensure a kill when they encountered Japanese Type 95s – the armour-piercing rounds punched right through them so easily that they failed to destroy them.)

PACIFIC THEATRE CAMPAIGN SUMMARY

While the main purpose of this book is to describe uniforms and equipment, a brief campaign summary may help readers put this material in context.

Philippines

The Japanese began amphibious landings on the islands culminating in the 22 December 1941 landing on Luzon. The half-trained Filipino army rapidly retreated and Manila fell on 26 December. Gen Douglas MacArthur made a planned withdrawal to the defence of the Bataan peninsula. The combined Filipino/US defenders were slowly pushed back and finally forced to surrender on 9 April 1942. The fortified island of Corregidor held out until Japanese amphibious assaults forced surrender on 6 May. MacArthur had failed to properly victual Bataan and Corregidor, but the defence had cost the Japanese five precious months.

New Guinea

In the winter of 1942 the Australian 7th and US 32nd Divisions, fighting in some of the worst jungle terrain in the world, forced the Japanese back from Port Moresby and into the defence of Buna. With almost no armour or artillery, the Allies finally seized Buna in January 1943. The US lost 60% of their force to disease along with 2,700 battle casualties. After a year of fighting, enveloping US amphibious landings at Aitape/Hollandia in April 1944 defeated the Japanese 18th Army at a cost of just 5,000 men. The US 41st Division's capture of Biak island in June 1944 was among the last pitched battles of the campaign. Skillful combined Australian/US operations would continue in New Guinea until its final subjugation in August 1944.

Solomon Islands

The US Army joined the Marines in the battle for Guadalcanal in October 1942 with the deployment of the 23rd Division. By January 1943 the 25th Division along with the 2nd Marine and 23rd Divisions were on the offensive; by February the island was secure, for the loss of 6,000 US casualties and an additional 9,000 sick.

The Army landed on New Georgia in July 1943 with the 37th and 43rd Divisions; joined by the 25th Division, they overcame fierce resistance and secured the island by the end of August.

In November 1943, Marines seized a five-by-ten mile perimeter around Empress Augusta Bay on Bougainville. Defence of the newly won terrain was left to the 23rd and 37th Divisions. By mid-1944 the island was secured.

New Britain

With the strategic Rabaul at the north end of the island, the 1st Cavalry Division and US Marines landed at the south (Cape Gloucester) in December 1943. By March 1944 the 40th and 1st Marine Divisions had advanced up the coasts, but this had cost MacArthur over 2,000 casualties for little real gain. The Australians then took over and contained Rabaul. The 1st Cavalry Division had gone on to capture Los Negros island (Admiralties) in late February 44.

Leyte, 1944: these men use the packboards usually associated with mountain troops to carry gear through the jungle. The foreground GI appears to be hauling the special rubberised case for carrying electronics and other water-sensitive gear.

Aleutians

After receiving desert training, the 7th Division landed on the cold, wet Japanese-held island of Attu in May 1943. Rooting out the 2,500-man enemy garrison cost the 7th 1,700 battle casualties and 2,100 men to non-battle causes, especially trench foot. The Japanese finished the battle with *banzai* charges and only 29 men survived the fighting to be captured. A combined US/Canadian force (including the 1st Special Service Brigade) landed on nearby Kiska island in August 1943, to find that the 4,500-strong Japanese garrison had been evacuated in late July.

Gilberts/Marshalls/Marianas

The 27th Division seized Makin (Gilberts) in November 1943. In February 1944 the 7th Division landed on Kwajalein (Marshalls), seizing the island in a week for a loss of just under 1,000 men. Later in the month, the 27th Division landed on Eniwetok in support of the Marines with similar results. In June 1944 the 27th Division reinforced two Marine divisions in the bitter fighting for Saipan (Marianas). Almost 30 days of fanatical Japanese resistance ended on 13 July; US losses were 16,000 men. During the battle, the 27th's commander was relieved by the (Marine) corps commander for lack of aggressiveness – a conflict which probably had more to do with differences in tactics between the Army and Marines than anything else. Guam (Marianas) fell to the Marines and the 77th Division in July 1944.

Philippines

The 1st Marine and 81st Divisions made the preliminary landings on the Palaus (Peleliu) in September 1944; fierce fighting cost the Marines 6,500 and the 81st 3,300 men. MacArthur's first landings in the Philippines hit Leyte unopposed in October. The Japanese rapidly fed in reinforcements, and the capture and pacification of the island would continue until VJ-Day, costing some 16,000 US casualties. MacArthur then landed on Luzon in January 1945. Gathering strength, the Army slowly began the drive to Manila and the nearby Clark Field airbase. The 275,000 Japanese troops commanded by the able Gen Yamashita mostly stayed in the rugged terrain of the north, waiting for a battle of attrition. Racing ahead with the 1st Cavalry and 37th Divisions, the US forces seized Clark Field and Manila after hard fighting, especially in the city; Manila fell on 4 March 1945. Corregidor would fall to a daring airborne and amphibious assault on 27 February. Until VJ-Day MacArthur continued to expend his forces on reducing the Japanese on the various islands of the Philippines archipelago and preparing for the assault on Japan. US losses in the Philippines were 64,000, with an additional 100,000-plus non-battle casualties.

Medical services

World War II saw huge advances in the treatment and evacuation of casualties, especially by US medical personnel. 'Wonder drugs' like penicillin, sulfa powder and morphine, and the ability to transfuse with stored blood, drastically reduced deaths due to infection and shock. Medics and sometimes GIs themselves carried sulfa powder and one-shot morphine ampules for immediate use in the foxhole. If a wounded GI could be safely evacuated for treatment – a big 'if' – his chances of survival were remarkably high, averaging 95.5% in 1941-45. About 75% even of stomach wounds, and an astonishing 95% of chest wounds, survived treatment. Even men with limbs blown off, or head wounds, survived more often than not – *if* they were evacuated to the rear areas quickly enough.

Disease, as always, was a major problem; during World War II as a whole, for every one man wounded in combat 27 were temporarily disabled by disease. In the Mediterranean and European theatres the Army's greatest single scourge was venereal disease. Malaria was also a serious problem in North Africa and Sicily. In the Pacific, VD was not a problem – but almost every other disease known to man was; the heavily jungled and malarial South-West Pacific was especially hazardous. Malaria was almost universal in combat areas, and dysentery, dengue fever and typhoid could cause debilitating fever and diarrhoea. For malaria the Allies produced Atabrine pills, which would suppress the symptoms; their side effects were that they turned the skin a yellowish hue – and were rumoured to cause sterility, which discouraged soldiers from taking them as ordered!

Wounds and serious diseases played a smaller part in the day-to-day miseries of the average GI than the results of the generally unhealthy environment. In the Pacific minor cuts, abrasions and insect bites rapidly became infected and often refused to heal without lengthy treatment. The chafing of constantly wet clothing caused widespread fungal skin diseases and ulcerations – generically called 'jungle rot'. Another medical problem not to be underestimated in the Pacific was simple heatstroke caused by high temperatures and extreme humidity.

As the Japanese gave priority to attacking aid stations and killing medics, the latter wore no red cross markings and commonly went armed. Aborigines in the South-West Pacific gave yeoman service in moving the wounded to the rear areas. Chaplains were also commonly to be found serving alongside medics.

(In the European theatre German troops generally did not fire deliberately on medical personnel. It was thus in the interests of stretcher bearers and medics to be distinguished in combat by the wearing of the red cross armband, and red cross markings on white disks or other shapes on their helmets.)

Japan, 1945: soldiers of the 'Americal' Division – note shoulder patch worn on khakis by the lieutenant, far right – receive medals before they return to the States. The men wear HBTs and helmet liners; NCO stripes began to reappear after VJ-Day.

DIVISIONAL CAMPAIGN SERVICE and shoulder patches

 6th Infantry Division ('Sight-seeing Sixth'). New Guinea, Philippines. Red six-point star.

 7th Infantry Division ('Hourglass'). Attu, Kwajalein, Leyte, Okinawa. Black diabolo on red disk.

 11th Airborne Division ('Angels'). Leyte, Manila, Cavite (Philippines). Blue shield under blue AIRBORNE arc; white winged circle surrounding red disk with white '11'.

 23rd Infantry Division ('Americal'). Guadalcanal, Bougainville, Cebu (Philippines). Southern Cross in white stars on blue shield.

 24th Infantry Division ('Victory'). New Guinea, Philippines. Green taro leaf edged yellow, on red disk edged black.

 25th Infantry Division ('Tropical Lightning'). Guadalcanal, New Georgia, Philippines. Yellow lightning bolt on red taro leaf edged yellow.

 27th Infantry Division ('New York'). Makin, Eniwetok, Saipan, Okinawa. Red 'NY' monogram and stars of constellation Orion, all on black disk.

 31st Infantry Division ('Dixie'). Philippines. Two opposed red 'Ds' in red circle, all on white disk.

 32nd Infantry Division ('Red Arrow'). New Guinea, Leyte. Upright red arrow with short horizontal crossbar.

 33rd Infantry Division ('Prairie'). Northern Luzon. Yellow cross on dark blue disk.

 37th Infantry Division ('Buckeyes'). Munda (New Georgia), Bougainville, Lingayen Gulf, Manila. Red disk edged white.

 38th Infantry Division ('Cyclone'). Bataan. White 'CY' monogram on shield halved blue (left) and red (right).

 40th Infantry Division ('Grizzly'). Admiralties, Philippines. Yellow sunburst on dark blue diamond.

 41st Infantry Division ('Sunset'). New Guinea, Marshalls, Mindanao, Palawan (Philippines). Yellow sun sinking into blue horizon against red sky.

 43rd Infantry Division ('Red Wing'). New Georgia, New Guinea, Luzon. Black grape leaf on red quatrefoil.

 77th Infantry Division ('Liberty'). Guam, Leyte, Okinawa. Yellow Statue of Liberty on dark blue tapered quadrilateral.

 81st Infantry Division ('Wildcat'). Angaur, Peleliu, Ulithi. Black cat facing left on khaki disk edged black.

 93rd Infantry Division ('Bloody Hand'). Bougainville, SW Pacific, Philippines. Horizon-blue Adrian helmet on black disk.

 96th Infantry Division ('Deadeyes'). Leyte, Okinawa. Blue diamond overlapping white diamond, all on horizontal khaki hexagon.

 1st Cavalry Division ('The First Team'). New Britain, Admiralties, Philippines. Black horsehead and diagonal stripe on yellow shield.

45

Okinawa

On 1 April 1945 the 10th Army landed four divisions on the 65-mile-long island of Okinawa, unopposed. Waiting in the hilly southern region were about 100,000 entrenched Japanese troops. Besides the 1st and 6th Marine Divisions, the 10th Army deployed the 7th, 27th, 77th and 96th Divisions. The US Navy fired over 600,000 large calibre shells in support. Southern Okinawa was taken yard by yard by riflemen, tanks and flamethrowers; the fighting was as savagely intense as in any previous island battle, and involved many more men on both sides, for longer – Okinawa did not finally fall until 21 June. With ferocious *kamikaze* attacks on the supporting fleet, Okinawa overall cost the US forces 50,000 casualties.

Okinawa, 1945: a rare capture of a Japanese soldier. This GI has a 'WP' grenade hanging from his M1936 suspenders; his helmet chinstrap is tucked up into the issue elastic neoprene band. Interestingly, he has three wristwatches on his left arm.

China-Burma-India

The US commitment to this theatre was in aircraft and logistics. Road-building by US Army Corps of Engineers and a massive aerial supply operation proved critical in supporting the Chinese war effort, and air support was extremely valuable to the British/Indian forces. Besides advisors and small units deployed to help the forming Chinese Army, the only US combat unit in the CBI was the 3,000-man 5307th Provisional Unit (known at various dates as 'Galahad', 'Merrill's Marauders', and 'Mars Task Force'). This was deployed to Burma in 1944, and helped British/Indian units seize the strategic airfield at Myitkyina.

Okinawa, May 1945: clustered round a jeep radio, weary GIs of 77th Division hear the news of the German surrender. Against the rain they wear the poncho, with its 'turtleneck' drawstring closure. For the men of the 'forgotten armies' in the Far East the war is emphatically not over yet.

THE PLATES: PACIFIC

A: THE PHILIPPINES, 1942

A1: Corporal, US Infantry, Philippines Division

This corporal is among the 23,000 US and Filipino regular troops defending the Philippines against the Japanese onslaught. His khaki cotton Class C ('chino') uniform is comfortable, but its light colour and lack of durability will be found wanting in combat; his rank chevrons are displayed on both sleeves. His helmet is the M1917A1 'dishpan' with the newer khaki chinstrap. Although a small number of M1 Garands were available in the Philippines, this soldier, like most, is armed with the standard M1903 Springfield bolt action rifle. Forsaken by the US, the 'Battling Bastards of Bataan' said that they had 'No Mama, no Papa, and no Uncle Sam'.

A2: 1st Lieutenant, US Cavalry

Officers' khaki shirts differed from the EMs' in having epaulettes (shoulder straps), and in the Philippines the pocket flaps were often customised as shown. This officer wears his rank bars at the end of his epaulettes and cut-out national and branch insignia on the collar points, as required in prewar regulations. This configuration was soon changed to wearing rank on the right shirt collar and branch on the left. This cavalryman has been assigned to an infantry unit and so wears the appropriate boots and leggings. His M1936 pistol belt and supenders support his .45cal semi-automatic pistol in a russet holster, web double-magazine pouch, World War I first aid pouch and (obscured here) canteen. His Thompson SMG is the prewar M1928 model with the distinctive top bolt and 50-round drum magazine.

A3: Filipino rifleman

Gen MacArthur was in the process of building up the new 100,000-man Filipino Army for the impending war with Japan which was anticipated to begin no sooner than mid-1942. Unprepared for war in late 1941, they performed poorly at first, but by the time the combined US/Filipino regulars were defending Bataan they had become viable soldiers. Filipino units were led by both Filipino and US officers. This well equipped man is armed with the World War I surplus M1917 (P17) rifle and helmet. If he survives the fighting to be captured he will probably have to endure the 'Bataan Death March' – during which more than 600 US and 5,000 Filipino soldiers would die of neglect, exhaustion and brutality. He will suffer unimaginable hardship as a prisoner in Japanese hands until liberation in 1945.

B: CALIFORNIA & HAWAII, 1942-43

B1: Private, Infantry, 1942

This soldier on sentry duty still awaits the issue of the new M1 helmet and M1 Garand rifle; he is also wearing a cavalry pattern cartridge belt, identified by its missing pouch on the front – pistol-armed horsemen used this spot to mount their two-magazine .45 pouch. Note the long World War I bayonet scabbard covered with canvas and leather. Brass tunic collar disks bearing 'US' and branch symbols were to be worn on the right and left shirt collar points respectively in 1942, but this order was soon rescinded. His tie is worn tucked into the shirt, as would be required throughout the war. In the autumn this man would revert to wearing the normal dark brown drab

Philippines, early 1942: an American officer in khaki chinos, with an M1928 Thompson, standing next to his Filipino counterpart. Both wear the M1917A1 helmet with web chinstrap; the Filipino officer wears medic's yoke suspenders, and a revolver in a civilian holster. US officers commonly served in the newly formed Filipino units. See Plate A.

wool uniform. When he is issued with a new M1 helmet and Garand it will almost certainly mean that his unit is about to go overseas.

B2: Captain (equivalent), Women's Army Auxiliary Corps, 1943

This officer, depicted immediately before the full incorporation of this organisation into the US Army as the Women's Army Corps, wears the first pattern officers' khaki cotton tunic; this was also available in gaberdine, similar to the male officer's khaki service tunic. The WAAC uniform design was a compromise; suggestions were requested from a number of leading civilian designers, but the final choice was predictably a 'committee compromise'. Note the unusual transverse shoulder straps, soon to be replaced by epaulettes – these bear metal rank insignia; the false breast pockets, and slash waist pockets; 'US' above branch badges on the collars and lapels; the issue shoulder bag, rayon stockings, and brown Oxford shoes. The hat was unofficially named after the female commander of the WAAC/WAC, Col (Director) Oveta Culp Hobby; here it still bears the WAAC's 'walking buzzard', soon to be replaced by the US Army officer's universal eagle badge.

B3: Captain, Field Artillery, 1943

Khaki coats and hats were used prewar but they were made of a moderately heavy cotton; in 1942 a slightly synthetic-looking gaberdine was also authorised for use in these coats. This coat and matching trousers would remain the standard until well after World War II. The single stripe of slightly contrasting cuff braid was the mark of officer status for all commissioned ranks. A khaki version of the conventional visored officer's service dress cap was also authorised, but this captain wears the khaki overseas cap, trimmed with mixed gold/black piping on the upper and front

Okinawa, 1945: three GIs from the 77th Division wearing typical uniforms and equipment of late war front line infantry. The medic (centre) has the standard medical pouches but not the yoke suspenders. Note (left) the World War I canteen, and the three-pocket grenade pouch hanging in front of his thigh. Both riflemen appear to be wearing the old M1928 pack, with two of the suspender straps looped together across their chests. At (right) the deep pocket of the second pattern HBT shirt shows well.

edge of the curtain; rank is worn at the front left. The national cypher is worn above branch insignia on the collar points and lapels; the latter sometimes displayed unit numbers, but these were not commonly available. His ribbons represent the American Campaign Medal and the Asiatic-Pacific Medal; the bronze fixture on the latter is a 'battle' star for service in New Guinea or on Guadalcanal.

C: GUADALCANAL, 1942-43

C1: Infantry private, 23rd Infantry Division, October 1942

The 'Americal' was the first Army division to be deployed to Guadalcanal in support of the battle-worn Marines. This private still wears the one-piece HBT overall suit; most men found this to be too hot, and hard to remove when (the very prevalent) dysentery came calling. He has dispensed with his leggings, and is typically accoutered for combat with the minimum of web equipment; note that like the figures on Plate A he still has the World War I patterns of canteen and first aid pouch on his rifle cartridge belt. Like the vast majority of GIs during the war he has decided not to buckle his helmet chinstrap; he would rather hold the helmet in place while running than risk a broken neck. Unlike his Marine comrades this GI is armed with the M1 Garand semi-automatic rifle; on Guadalcanal the Marines quickly saw the value of its high rate of fire, and 'obtained' as many as possible. He also carries a fragmentation grenade in his right breast pocket.

C2: Rifle grenadier, 25th Infantry Division, 1943

This 'sad sack' is wearing one of the handy new ponchos based on the USMC design; in its role as rainwear this green shelter-half, which had a myriad of uses, could be snapped along the edges to form loose sleeves, and covered both man and equipment. He is armed with the M1903A3 modification of the Springfield, the most discernible difference being the new placement of the rear sight; note also the rifle grenade launcher attachment at the muzzle. The short T-handled shovel of World War I was used throughout the war, although its (theoretical) replacement – the folding-head tool based on the German model – would soon arrive. The 25th 'Tropical Lightning' Division, with its prewar Regular

Army cadre, would win a Distinguished Unit Citation for its actions in the Guadalcanal campaign.

C3: Infantry sergeant, 23rd Infantry Division, 1943

Although he has tucked the shirt into the trousers, his first pattern HBT two-piece uniform is identifiable by its pleated breast pockets. Because its green colour faded quickly with use it was sometimes overdyed a blackish green. This NCO shows no insignia; he is armed with a M97 Winchester pump-action 12 gauge shotgun, a .45cal pistol, and an early war MkIIA1 fragmentation grenade painted yellow all over – this was soon reduced to a narrow yellow stripe around the top of the grenade body. Shotguns were used by the Army and Marines throughout the Pacific campaigns, but in very limited numbers and not without some controversy.

D: SOUTH-WEST PACIFIC, 1943-44

D1: Corporal machine gunner

An infantry battalion's heavy weapons company would normally have eight .30cal water-cooled M1917A1 machine guns. This GI cradles one of these weapons – which weighs 41lbs (18.6kg) with water in the jacket. The M1917A1 and the lighter air-cooled M1919 were functionally almost identical, though the more awkward tripod and the water jacket of the 1917 model allowed sustained defensive fire. The corporal section leader wears the later pattern HBT shirt with long, unpleated pockets, and the new HBT trousers with thigh cargo pockets (both the shirt and trouser pockets could hold the new K-ration box). He displays no rank insignia, and is identifiable only by his role as gunner, his pistol belt and holstered .45 automatic.

D2: Private second gunner

Like his crewmates he wears a second pattern HBT shirt. The blackened metal '13-star' buttons used on HBTs – sometimes known as the 'Starburst of Freedom' design – were sometimes later replaced by standard drab green plastic buttons. While not popular, this large-mesh helmet netting would last most of the war as an issue item. His footwear is the latest in specially designed jungle boots; while lacking in support their lightness and quick drying made them attractive to many GIs. (An ankle-length version was also seen in use.) The Browning tripod weighs 52lbs (23.6kg); he also carries an all-purpose ammunition bag (its LTD fasteners suggesting a locally made 'custom' example), an M1 carbine and its two-magazine pouch, and an entrenching tool.

D3: Private ammunition bearer
Two or more men would be assigned to carry ammunition for a machine gun; each can carried 250 belted rounds and weighed 5lbs (.2kg). Old World War I vintage wooden boxes were also still in limited use, but this steel box was the standard (and has remained in US Army use with few changes to this day). This GI is wearing the standard mid-war HBTs – unusually, with leggings – and is using one of several similar patterns of issue machete to cut trail. Clips for his Garand are carried in his web rifle belt and a use-and-throw-away cotton bandoleer; the bayonet would hang on his left hip. These M1936 web suspenders were commonly discarded in the Pacific; here he has a MkIIA1 grenade fixed to one – GIs sometimes used tape to secure them.

E: CHOWTIME, 1943-44
E1: Sniper of an infantry unit
This sniper wears the one-piece M1942 camouflaged suit, and the M1941 billed soft fatigue cap – a very popular item, and sometimes seen worn under the helmet. The one-piece suit was the first special jungle uniform issued, but like its HBT green counterpart it proved too hot and too awkward – when heading for the latrine the GI had to remove his web equipment and shrug the top half of the suit right down. The camouflage pattern of green and brown spots on a drab straw-coloured ground was also somewhat easy to spot when the wearer moved. Nevertheless, for snipers – who moved very little when working – the suit proved useful. This GI is armed with the M1903A4 with a Weaver 2.5 x scope sight. He carries a lightweight 60-round bandoleer for extra ammunition; behind him is the new M1943 jungle pack.

E2: Medical orderly, 93rd Infantry Division
This medic from an African-American unit wears the same one-piece camouflage suit as E1; it was in common issue in 1943. His footwear are the canvas and rubber jungle boots; and his floppy hat is the later green HBT version of the earlier 1940 khaki 'Daisy Mae'. His pair of medical pouches are supported by special yoke suspenders. This soldier is unarmed, although medics commonly armed themselves in

the Pacific theatre due to the Japanese habit of targeting them; for the same reason he displays no red cross insignia. The carry-all bag at his feet, designed to hold a steel ammunition box, was used for many different purposes in the field. African-Americans served in segregated support units throughout the Army, but one all-black division – the 93rd, which had distinguished itself under French Army command in World War I – served in the Pacific.

E3: Staff sergeant of a Tank Battalion
This staff sergeant wears the one-piece HBT suit intended for mechanics and vehicle crews. As was common with HBTs – but rare in the Pacific – he has inked his rank on to the sleeves of his coverall. He wears the first pattern of the .45 pistol shoulder holster, which was intended for the use of tankers and drivers. In his fibre and leather tank crew helmet he carries K-ration boxes, the breakfast, dinner and supper meals marked and colour-coded.

US tanks could easily handle Japanese tanks, but the enemy's 47mm anti-tank gun could knock out a Sherman from the side; suicide attacks by sappers with pole or satchel charges and anti-tank grenades were also a serious threat. Some of the Army tank and tank destroyer units which saw action in the Pacific included:

SW Pacific: *Bougainville, 1944* 754th Tk Bn; *Hollandia, New Guinea, 1944* 4th Tk Bn, 632nd TD Bn (M10) *Biak* 603rd Sep.Tk Co.

Central Pacific: *Makin, Nov 1943* 193rd Tk Bn (M3 Lee); *Marshalls, Feb 1944* 767th Tk Bn (M4A1, M5A1, M10, flamethrower tanks); 766th Tk Bn; *Marianas, June 1944 – Saipan* 762nd, 766th Tk Bns *Guam* 706th Tk Bn; *Palau Islands, Sept 1944* 710th Tk Bn, 819th TD Bn (M10); *Philippines, Dec 1944-Feb 1945* 44th, 716th, 754th Tk Bns, 632nd (M10), 637th (M18) TD Bns.

Okinawa: 706th, 711th, 713th, 715th Tk Bns.

F: PHILIPPINES, 1944-45
F1: Officer, Ranger or Scout unit
This officer wears the newly available two-piece version of the M1942 camouflage jungle uniform. By the final year of the war most GIs received – and preferred – the standard green HBTs, and use of the camouflage uniform became uncommon. Long range reconnaissance scouts did use this uniform quite frequently, however, and preferred the soft fatigue cap to the steel helmet. This man wears no insignia, but is probably an officer in the 6th Ranger Battalion, or perhaps a member of the 6th Army's small 'Alamo Scouts'

This unusual photo of the commander and staff of the 6th Ranger Bn in a rear area shows rank insignia and camouflage helmet covers being worn. In combat no rank would be displayed, and billed soft caps were preferred by the Rangers. The CO (front) appears to be wearing paratrooper boots. The 6th Rangers were constituted in 1944 and served with distinction in the Philippines.

Burma, 1944: dog handlers of BrigGen Frank D.Merrill's 5307th Composite Unit ('Merrill's Marauders', later Mars Task Force) – cf Plate F. The GI with the carbine has padded the straps of his camouflage jungle pack. The Thompson gunner (left) wears the rubber and canvas jungle boots, and a soft billed cap under his helmet; note his dog's first aid pouch. For their third mission in April 1944 the 5307th comprised H Force (Col Hunter) with 1st Bn divided into Red and White Combat Teams, plus the Chinese 150th Regt; M Force (LtCol McGee) with 2nd Bn and 300 local Kachin guerrillas; and K Force (Col Kinnison) with 3rd Bn divided into Orange and Khaki Combat Teams, plus the Chinese 88th Regiment.

unit. He wears the newly issued buckle boots, which would rapidly become the common issue footwear in this last year of the war. Magazine pouches for his M1 carbine are carried on his pistol belt and the butt of the weapon. Instead of an issue machete he carries a local bolo for cutting trail through the jungle.

F2: Battalion commander, 11th Airborne Division

The Corcoran paratrooper boots are the only features that might identify this man as Airborne – for ground combat he has removed the special chin harness from his helmet liner. Nor does he wear any visible insignia to mark him as a lieutenant-colonel or major commanding a battalion, though his shoulder-holstered pistol suggests that he is an officer. This sort of smudgy helmet camouflage pattern was painted on by several units in the last year of the war. His M3 fighting knife will soon be replaced by the M1 carbine bayonet; and note the large green pouch of the jungle first aid kit.

The small 11th Airborne Division retained its 8,200-man establishment throughout the war; it first saw action as reinforcements on Leyte in November 1944. MacArthur also had at his disposal the independent 503rd Parachute Infantry Regiment, which jumped at Nadzab (1943), Noemfoor (1944), and – most famously – at Corregidor in February 1945.

F3: Private, 26th Quartermaster War Dog Platoon

This left-handed private listening to a SCR 536 'handie-talkie' radio appears to be serving as a HQ runner. He too has a camouflage-painted helmet, and wears a late pattern HBT shirt, but still has the older issue ankle boots of 1941, with toecaps, and trousers without cargo pockets worn rolled over web leggings. He is armed with an M1 Garand and a MkIIA1 'pineapple' grenade. An immediate-use clip of Garand rounds was often carried jammed on to a web suspender, as here; interestingly, this GI has a complete clip

of red-tipped tracer rounds (black tips identified armour-piercing ammunition). The platoon/company level SCR 536 (Set, Complete Radio) AM radio had a range of about two miles and was preset to a single frequency. It had no external switches and was turned on simply by extending the antenna.

Medium-sized dogs from one to five years old, measuring 20ins (50.8cm) at the shoulder and weighing at least 50lbs (22.7kg) could be 'recruited' for service in the 'K9' Corps; German Shepherds were the preferred breed, though the Marines liked Dobermans. Interestingly, the Quartermaster Corps provided both the dogs and their handlers. War dogs were trained for use as scouts, couriers, pack animals and to guard POWs. After hard service many dogs were found to be too sensitive to prolonged artillery fire, with disease (heartworm) and fatigue also taking a toll. (Dogs were not eligible for the Purple Heart...)

G: OKINAWA, 1945

G1: BAR gunner, 77th Infantry Division

The BAR – here stripped of all its attachments – provided the basis of the rifle squad's firepower, and was a key player in the bunker-busting teams used in the last year of the war. Dressed in standard late war HBTs, this BAR man also wears the new buckle boots now commonly issued. His helmet shows the 77th Division's 'Lady Liberty' insignia worn on Okinawa; this has been illustrated as a plain white outline, but close-up photos (e.g. one of a company commander, Capt Buckner M.Creel, receiving the Silver Star) show that at least some helmets carried the full yellow-on-blue symbol on the white ground on both sides. Except for camouflage, markings of any kind on helmets in the Pacific were rare, although rank symbols were occasionaly painted on the back. At one time men of the 27th Division also displayed a formation symbol, a white outline parallelogram on the left side of green-and-black camouflaged helmets. Also to be noted here is the elastic helmet band commonly issued in the last year of the war. Metal-framed spectacles with almost oval lenses were standard issue to GIs who needed them.

G2: Flamethrower operator, 77th Infantry Division
This combat engineer dressed in late war HBTs wields the M1A1 flamethrower; he needs to use both hands and to brace himself when firing or he might be knocked over by the 'recoil' force of the nitrogen propelling the napalm fuel.

G3: Infantry private, US Marine Corps
Marines and GIs fought side by side on Guadalcanal, at Cape Gloucester, on Saipan and Okinawa, and although rivalry was often intense the Army's 77th Division enjoyed an unusually good relationship with the USMC. This 'lost' Marine – at 18-20 years old, about eight or ten years younger than the average 77th Division GI – has been volunteered to join an Army unit for the time being as an assistant to a flamethrower man. The rifle-armed assistant helped protect the laden operator; turned on the fuel and propellant tanks for him when going into combat; and by this date would carry a 5gal jerrycan of napalm fuel to reload the flamethrower.

Items that indicate this man's Marine identity are the standard USMC HBTs – known as utilities or dungarees – with the distinctive 'USMC' and eagle, globe and anchor pocket stencil, the Marines' unique camouflage helmet cover, and the K-bar fighting knife. Marines had no access to buckle boots so this man wears the issue 'rough-out' low quarter boots. In a pocket he should be carrying a 'WP' grenade for throwing in case the lighting mechanism on the flamethrower muzzle fails to ignite the fuel.

H: MISCELLANEOUS

H1: Rifleman, Kiska Task Force; Aleutians, summer 1943
Though technically serving in the Pacific theatre, this GI is necessarily kitted out for winter conditions – the Aleutians lie far north in the Bering Sea. He wears bib-fronted, wool-lined, cotton canvas tanker's winter trousers under his 'M1941' Parsons jacket. His boots are either from an early trials batch of M1944 shoepacs, or the privately purchased civilian type on which these were modelled. Winter overboots, though dry and warm, could make the feet first sweat, then freeze. Members of the Kiska Task Force apparently wore the knife shoulder patch on whichever sleeve they liked. Attu fell to the 7th Division after a stiff fight, but although the Japanese had already evacuated Kiska the island still cost the US Army 2,000 casualties due to foot disorders and sickness. A variety of cold weather gear was tried out in this campaign, including mackinaws and the longer arctic model of the Parsons jacket.

H2: Supply sergeant, South-West Pacific, 1943
This rear area NCO is dressed for comfort in a khaki shirt and shorts. It was very unusual to see combat GIs wearing shorts, since any scratches or insect bites almost invariably became infected (artillerymen sometimes wore shorts, but they were more static). Nearby is the early war issue pith helmet, but he is wearing a semi-official 'swing' soft cap, the slightly longer-billed version of the M1941 favoured by the

Okinawa, 1945: this veteran infantryman from the 96th Division is – typically – as lightly equipped for combat as possible. He has only his rifle, a cartridge belt, a first aid pouch and an (empty) canteen carrier visible; he might add a poncho and a grenade.

11th Airborne Division. His boots are the Australian-made hobnailed version of the low quarter 'service shoes'. On his pistol belt are a compass pouch, a canteen and a holstered revolver – either a M1917 .45cal or, more likely, a Smith & Wesson .38 Model 10.

H3: First sergeant, 8th Army Headquarters; Japan, late 1945
In the chilly Japanese autumn this veteran NCO, enjoying the fruits of victory, wears his brown drab wool service uniform. The overseas cap is piped in infantry light blue. The 'Ike' jacket – offically the M1944 OD wool field jacket – was very popular as a Class A walking-out dress, and rapidly supplanted the four-pocket wool coat whenever it could be acquired. On his right and left collar points respectively he wears the EMs' brass disks bearing 'US' and the crossed rifles of his branch. This prewar regular soldier has completed two enlistments and has been overseas for 2.5 years, as shown by the diagonal and straight 'hash marks' (the latter for six months each) on his left forearm. His current posting to 8th Army HQ is shown by his left shoulder patch; on his right shoulder he is allowed to continue to wear the patch of the 25th 'Tropical Lightning' Division (inset, 3a) in which he served in combat. Below the blue and silver Combat Infantryman's Badge on his left breast his ribbons include the Bronze Star with 'V' for valour, and the Asiatic-Pacific campaign ribbon with four battle stars. Obscured here, he would wear above his right pocket the blue Distinguished Unit Citation (renamed postwar the Presidential Unit Citation).

THE MEDITERRANEAN

THE US ARMY that sailed for the Mediterranean theatre in late 1942 was a very untried force. With the American public impatient for action against Nazi Germany it was politically necessary to get into the war soon. The Allied landings in Vichy North Africa, and especially the fighting which followed in Tunisia, blooded the green American troops and their leaders. With momentum in the Mediterranean and landings in France postponed until 1944, the British general staff were instrumental in persuading the other Allies to carry the war into Sicily and Italy in mid-1943. This fighting precipitated the collapse of the first of the Axis powers; Italy first surrendered, and then joined the Allied cause. The campaigns gave both the US Army and Navy valuable experience in amphibious warfare, lessons which would be put to good effect in Normandy in June 1944. But that concentration on the northern front limited the resources available in Italy; and the continued expenditure of Allied lives and equipment in the Italian mountains in 1944/45 would ultimately prove to be a strategic dead end.

Three of the best organisations in the US Army served in the Italian theatre. Interestingly, the 442nd (Nisei) Regiment, 1st Special Service Force and 10th Mountain Division were all specialised units that Gen Eisenhower refused for service in France. General Mark Clark's US 5th Army in Italy also received the first all-draftee 85th and 88th Divisions, and the African-American 92nd Division.

The US Army would maintain about six-plus divisions in 'the boot' until VE-Day, serving alongside British, Canadian, Indian, New Zealand, South African, Polish, French, North African, Brazilian and 'Co-Belligerent' Italian forces against the stubbornly brilliant fighting retreat of the Wehrmacht, which was conducted for most of the campaign by Field-Marshal Albert Kesselring.

At sea, November 1942: an unarmed chaplain prepares for the 'Operation Torch' landings in French North Africa. He wears the OD wool shirt and trousers common to all GIs, with a flag shoulder patch; a leather-bottomed musette bag on his right hip, and the large haversack for the service gasmask. He has the Christian cross on his left collar, and seems to wear his priest's narrow purple 'stole' tied around his left arm as identification.

UNIFORMS

Cold weather clothing

The Army began the war with essentially World War I style winter clothing. Drab wool shirts and trousers with the short 'M1941' or 'Parsons' field jacket were standard wear. For really cold weather the shin-length, double-breasted overcoat in 32oz drab wool was the usual issue. The coat had a large roll collar, epaulettes, rear expansion pleats and integral half-belt, and two 'slash' (internal) side pockets. It used general service brass eagle buttons for most of the war, although green plastic buttons replaced these later. Shortages of more specialised cold weather gear at the front and supply incompetence – particularly in

Belgium and France in 1944 – forced combat GIs to fall back on this monster overcoat throughout the last winter of the war. It was warm and water-resistant, but it was heavy. Unless literally in the dead of winter, troops tried to avoid wearing it. (Truck drivers sometimes used the overcoat with the skirt cut off at the hip for increased convenience.) In poor light it also gave the wearer the unfortunate silhouette of the overcoat worn by many German troops. It remained the service dress overcoat throughout the war; when appropriate, NCOs' rank stripes were worn on both sleeves in olive drab (OD) felt on black. The long button-front raincoat was also issued for winter use by front line troops.

Another hold-over from World War I was the mackinaw. Three versions of this coat were used in World War II, all thigh-length, double-breasted, belted coats with shawl collars. Comfortable and well-liked, they were a bit bulky for combat use, though somewhat more common among combat officers; they were especially popular among truck drivers. All the patterns had a water-repellant khaki/light green 10oz cotton duck exterior similar to that of the lighter Parsons field jacket, and a 26–30oz drab wool lining. The pre-war mackinaw had a wool-faced collar; the two M1941/42 versions had cloth collars. All had plain drab plastic buttons, a strapped cuff and two flapped internal waist pockets. The M1941/42 versions were slightly lighter in construction and thus less warm; the last version dispensed with the integral belt.

A buttoned knee-length arctic coat/parka was also available at the outbreak of the war. Rarely seen, this was essentially a longer version of

Officers at the 19th Engineer Regt command post near the Rapido River, January 1944; one wears the first pattern mackinaw with wool-faced collar. The radioman at left wears the II Corps patch above his technical corporal's rank badge. The pole aerial is the old cavalry type, designed to be carried like a lance by a mounted man.

The Pulitzer Prize-winning correspondent Ernie Pyle (right), wearing a mackinaw and a knit jeep cap with goggles, chatting with tank crewmen in Italy; note the cold weather 'tanker's' jacket at left. Pyle was widely admired as a writer with the common touch, who served as an unofficial spokesman for the GI to the folks back home. After VE-Day he served in the Pacific, and was with the 77th Division when he was killed in action on Ie Shima, Okinawa.

A Forceman of the FSSF, his shoulder patch 'blotted' by the censor, wearing the new M1943 field jacket and mountain trousers – the buttons on the cargo pocket distinguish these from the snap-fastened Airborne equivalent. Visible weapons are a Thompson, a .45 pistol and a Mk II grenade. He wears a web ten-pocket rifle belt.

the mackinaw but fur-lined, with a hood but without the belt. It was, however, too bulky for all but the coldest climate. For the winter of 1944/45 a hooded, fur-lined version of the arctic parka was becoming available; this had an external belt similar to that of the mountain troops' field jacket (see Plate G1). Although it is rarely seen in photos, some do show it worn by Generals Patton and Bradley.

Developed early in the war as a winter combat uniform, the Army wool-lined, bibbed overalls and short windcheater-style jacket had much to recommend them. Like the mackinaw, the winter combat trousers were of windproof and water-repellant cotton duck lined with drab blanket-weight wool; they had a bibbed front which extended up the chest, with suspenders. They featured a zipper down the front, zippers on the hips to access inside trouser pockets, and a 'quick piss' zipper on the lower front. The bibbed trousers were intended to be worn over regular woollen trousers and a shirt.

The winter combat ('tanker's') jacket had knit cuffs, waist and neck, and slash 'handwarmer' internal front pockets. The jacket had 'bi-swing' expanding back panels and no epaulettes. (I believe that a small number of an earlier version of the jacket were produced with flapped pockets and epaulettes.) With its knit neck, waist and cuffs this garment was warmer than the M1941 Parsons jacket, and was a highly prized item among all combat GIs. The bibbed trousers were also in demand, although rather bulky for infantry use. Officers of all ranks commonly wore the tanker jacket, with rank insignia pinned onto the shoulders or on custom-fitted epaulettes. Both the jacket and trousers were generally set aside for armoured vehicle personnel, and were usually seen worn by tankers and sometimes by their attendant armoured infantrymen.

The Army Quartermaster developed most of the new cold weather uniforms on the 'layering' principle; and OD knit wool sweaters certainly fitted into that scheme. Sleeved and sleeveless pullovers were common.

Near Rome, June 1944: Medics of the 1st Special Service Force watch a comrade being loaded into a medical evacuation halftrack. Note their paratrooper boots and mountain trousers, characteristic of the FSSF (see Plate E3).

The sleeved pullover with a low collar and a five-button chest closure was usually a bit tighter fitting and was worn both over and under shirts. Also available for winter use by 1943 were a woollen knit 'burglar's' toque, and heavier 18oz drab wool trousers.

Light brown leather work gloves were used in the Army. For winter use knit OD/drab green gloves were issued. Fingered gloves were the more common, including a version with brown leather palms and fingers. Knit mittens with separate 'trigger fingers', and canvas/leather overmittens, were also to be seen. A drab/OD woollen scarf was also widely used throughout the war.

Due to perpetual shortages, winter overshoes and so-called 'shoepacs' were a seasonal headache for the Army. Trench foot and frozen feet took a serious toll as a result. The 5th Army in Italy lost about 20% of its manpower during the winter of 1943/44 due to trench foot. During the December 1944 Battle of the Bulge in Belgium the losses due to foot problems were about 40% of the total.

The overshoes mainly issued in 1943/44 were the black canvas and rubber M1942 model with four metal clip buckles at the front, about 10ins high at the ankle. This overshoe suffered from the separation of the rubber sole from the canvas upper. An improved five-buckle version came out late in the war. Also available early in the war was the rubber and leather 16in high lace-up 'Blucher' boot made of mostly greased leather. For troops on the move this boot was found to cause serious foot problems, and did not last. About the best – or least inadequate – winter boot was the M1944 steel-shanked 'shoepac'. This had a rubber bottom and leather top, was 12ins high, and was efficiently waterproofed.

All of these boots gave adequate warmth when worn with woollen standard and ski socks; the M1944 used a fibre insert. None of them really answered the needs of troops involved in winter marching.

Officers in combat had access to all the same winter clothing as the EMs. On rare occasions they were to be seen on the battlefield using the officer's OD green trenchcoat. Most company grade officers preferred tanker jackets, M1943 four-pocket combat jackets or mackinaws.

In service dress, several models of trenchcoat and a shawl-collar mackinaw-style beige wool coat were to be seen used by officers. General officers were, by custom, allowed a wide latitude in their choice of uniform. Generals overseas were to be seen in the whole variety of combat jackets, including Air Corps leather and nylon flight jackets. Custom-cut or modified coats were also seen. By 1944/45 the two or three patterns of the short blouse-style 'Ike jacket' – M1944 OD wool field jacket – were in fashion among generals and senior officers, especially staff and non-divisional types. (The old M1904 brass-buckled 'US' black leather belt was also seen in use, especially by Gen Patton. This belt is still a prerogative of general officers in the US Army to this day.)

Mountain troops' uniforms

The 1st Special Service Force and the 10th Mountain Division (see below under Organisation) had a significant number of items specially developed for their use. Winter coats were among the most obvious special issue items.

OPPOSITE **91st Division GI displaying newly issued M1944 'shoepacs', M1943 jacket (still with its makers' and issue tags stapled on), and wool sleeping bag with cover. Troops in Italy in 1944 generally received a timely issue of winter gear; many GIs in France had to wait until January 1945 for theirs.**

However desirable sleeping bags are, to the frontline soldier they were almost unusable. GIs had to be free to leap to their weapons and fighting positions, and could not afford the time to get out of a bag and put their boots on again. The old drab wool blanket (M1934) with bound edges, and a rain poncho were probably the best sleeping gear available to combat GIs. The bag used by the Army essentially looked like a wool blanket folded over with a zipper added; it was a 'mummy'-style bag with cloth tapes at the feet to tie up the roll and a hooded headpiece at the top. It sometimes came with an OD water-resistant outer shell. This bag could be ingeniously modified by GIs in winter by cutting arm holes and wearing it under a jacket with the hood retained. A rarely-seen goose down mummy bag was also available for arctic use.

Men of the FSSF were issued just about every boot then made for the Army. This line-up under a bunk at Ft Harrison, Montana, in 1943 shows (left to right) low-quarter dress shoes, two pairs of ankle-length service shoes, mountain-ski boots, jump boots, and four-clip cold weather overshoes.

The Army issue M1941 drab cotton poplin anorak was based on European mountain wear. The general pattern was a thigh-length, hooded, pullover jacket with two angled 'handwarmer' chest pockets. It had drawstring neck and wrist closures and was fully reversible to white. Different versions of this came with or without buttoned or unbuttoned pocket flaps. A later version had a three-button neck opening.

The first type (ski) anorak had a fur-trimmed hood and cuffs. A white pile liner with knit cuffs was developed to add real warmth; in the snow, this pile lining could be worn as an outer coat. Pile-lined arctic parkas were also used by the mountain troops.

The M1942 mountain coat was specially designed for use by the Mountain Division. It was a close cousin of the M1943 combat jacket, and appears at first glance to be the same garment. It was made of a similar OD green cotton and had two expandable breast pockets and two internal skirt pockets. The lower pockets had an exposed OD plastic button, as did the flap covering the zipper front of the jacket. The mountain jacket had a detachable hood but no epaulettes. Its most noticeable features were the exposed web belt and buckle, and especially the integral hump-backed 'pack'. The pack had a zippered side access, and the waistbelt helped hold it down when it was folded and not in use. An interior strapping arrangement around the arms and shoulders supported the integral pack when it was extended and in use (see Plate G3).

The M1942 mountain trousers were simply stout OD cotton pants with tapered cuffs and thigh cargo pockets. They had angled and zippered front pockets and flapped rear pockets as well as the buttoned cargo pockets. The trousers had both buttons for suspenders and belt loops. The tapered cuffs had elastic strapping for the instep. Drab wool M1941 ski trousers were also issued. These had a broad waistband closed with three buttons, and the tapered cuffs also had elastics fitted. Other unusual items that might be seen in use by the 10th Mountain or the 1st SSF included skis, snowshoes, rucksacks, and short European-style mountain boots and gaiters.

Italy, 1944: a 34th Division MP directing traffic under shellfire, ready to duck at any moment. He appears to wear the pile liner for the M1943 jacket turned inside out – the outside was cotton duck.

Military Police usually came in two flavours: divisional MPs, and the rear echelon corps and army level MPs. Rear echelon MPs were in charge of enforcing regulations and discipline. They could 'ticket' (fine) or arrest malefactors for e.g. public drunkenness, uniform infractions, or any criminal activity; traffic control and general security were also common responsibilities. Divisional MPs handled traffic, area security, POWs and discipline. They operated close enough to the front to be at risk, and their control of road junctions under artillery fire could be hazardous. Divisional MPs were held in high regard by infantrymen, and as 5th Army veteran Bill Mauldin states, 'If an MP wearing the insignia of the dogface's own outfit tells him to do something, the doggie usually listens.'

Airborne troops' uniform

After experiments with HBT and green sateen 'balloon cloth' jumpsuits with patch zippered pockets, a khaki cotton twill two-piece jumpsuit was selected. Unlike the German and British airborne, the US Army decided to forgo a jump oversmock. The US paratroops were expected to jump with their weapons and almost all of their equipment on their person (i.e. mostly in their pockets). After a test 'M1941 jump uniform' was created in the Fort Benning tailors' shop, an improved M1942 suit was approved; this was made of a khaki/tan windproof and water-repellant cotton cloth.

The M1942 had four patch cargo pockets with inverted pleats and flaps closed with two smooth press studs. The zipped-front jacket also featured an integral belt, epaulettes, a gusset up the spine and bi-swing rear shoulders. The matching trousers had both regular side seam and inverted-pleat thigh cargo pockets; the inseam had cloth leg tapes to tie down pockets and equipment. The trouser legs were tapered to fit into the jumpboots.

For headgear, A-2 and A-8 cloth flight toques were first used, soon to be replaced by football-style Riddell crash helmets. The general issue steel pot helmet came next, with its special webbing in the liner (M1C) to suspend a leather-cupped chinstrap. Woollen knit jeep caps ('beanies') were commonly worn to cushion the helmet for landing.

Footwear was based on an 11-eyelet high-top boot probably first used by civilian 'smoke jumpers'. This boot had a strap and buckle for ankle support; the modified GI version soon produced was a russet leather 11-eyelet boot minus the ankle strap, with a toecap, bevelled front sole edges, and a partial rubber tread for moving across aircraft floors. Corcoran was the most famous of several manufacturers, and this very successful and popular boot soon acquired that generic nickname. The jump boots were commonly worn by the 1st SSF, who had originally been jump-trained, and also by any other officers and GIs lucky enough to obtain them.

In Europe the M1942 jump uniform was frequently modified by adding knee and elbow reinforcement patches (sometimes padded). The light colour was also considered a problem by some units, who over-sprayed the uniform with stripes of OD or black paint. By the latter part of 1944 the Army began issuing the new general issue M1943 OD four-pocket combat jackets and buckle boots to paratroopers. The new jacket was accepted, but jump boots were retained if at all possible. Paratroops also received M1943 OD trousers with thigh cargo pockets added – a field modification.

Besides uniforms, other items peculiar to Airborne troops were M2 switchblade knives, World War I brass knuckleduster trench knives, M1A1 folding-stock carbines, and special Air Corps-produced web belt pouches of several patterns. US paratroopers in 1944 also jumped with a special cloth parachute first aid packet which included a tourniquet, field dressing and morphine syrette; this was usually attached to a shoulder strap or the helmet.

Italy, 1944: this Pfc wears a tanker's jacket and buckle boots; note also the folding-head shovel, based on a German model. He uses an SCR 300 radio to keep his company commander in touch with battalion; 'SCR' stands for 'Set, Complete Radio' – i.e. combining receiver and transmitter – rather than 'Signal Corps Radio' as sometimes stated.

The US Army was lavishly supplied with radio sets; most tactical radios were FM. The SCR 194/195/300 series backpack radios, termed 'Walkie-Talkies', were used at battalion and company level and had a range of about five miles. The hand-held SCR 536 or 'Handie-Talkie' was used at platoon level, with a range of about a mile (under good conditions – sometimes it was said to be easier to just shout). Most tanks and command jeeps had radios. The availability of radios was one of the key factors allowing mobile and decentralised tactics; the US Army especially could co-ordinate infantry and tank movement with artillery support to an unprecedented degree.

The special insignia of the US Airborne are too extensive to cover here, but the silver jump wings and overseas hat Airborne patch were the most obvious (see Osprey Elite 31, *US Army Airborne 1940-90* by Gordon Rottman and Ronald Volstad).

M1943 combat uniform

The hip-length M1943 combat jacket (PQD370) was inspired by the M1942 paratroop jacket. It was made of an OD green smooth sateen cotton shell with cotton lining. The jacket had two patch breast pockets and two internal skirt pockets, epaulettes, concealed plastic buttons, and a drawstring waist for better fitting. The M1943 was first tested at Anzio by the 3rd Division, and was soon in great demand. The large pocket arrangement was especially admired, and GIs found they could almost fight without web gear by using the voluminous pockets.

Complaints were based on the fact the jacket was neither waterproof nor warm enough. For winter wear it was always intended to be used with a liner or a sweater. The M1943 jacket liner or pile field jacket was a artificial (mohair/alpaca) pile fur garment with a light chocolate brown cotton exterior and knit cuffs and collar. It had two slash pockets, and closed with six plastic buttons and cloth loops. The simple liner was well liked, and was often used as a separate garment or with the parka. It is not generally appreciated that the wool 'Ike' jacket was also intended to be worn in combination with the M1943 jacket (though it rarely was). GIs were also seen to wear the M1941 Parsons jacket under the M1943. A detachable hood that could be worn over or under the helmet was also a part of the M1943 uniform.

The M1943 was rapidly accepted by the 5th Army in Italy but refused by the ETO until late in 1944. The M1943 jacket is now seen as perhaps the best combat uniform to come out of the war, and is emulated by most modern combat jackets. Its line of descent to the US Army's current camouflaged BDU is evident to this day.

Also issued with the new jacket were the M1943 OD green sateen cotton cloth over-trousers (PQD371). These were to be worn over wool trousers, and had side seam and rear slash pockets along with a small watch pocket in the right front. They also featured both belt loops and suspender buttons. GIs sometimes modified these trousers by adding thigh cargo pockets.

ORGANISATION

'Heavy' and 'Light' Armored Divisions

The Army was still experimenting with armoured unit organisations when the German Panzers overran France. By July 1940 the 1st and 2nd Armored Divisions had been organised as assets of an Armored Corps. Originally these divisions each had two light tank regiments and

1942 (Heavy) Armored Division

- Armored Regt
  - Armored Bn
- Infantry Regt
  - Infantry Bn
- Artillery Bn
- Ordnance, Supply, Medical, etc.
- Armored Recon Bn
- Signal Co
- Engineer Bn

one medium. By 1942 the Armored Division consisted of two tank regiments of three battalions each, and a mechanised infantry regiment also of three battalions. The division also had a reconnaissance battalion of light tanks and armoured cars, and three self-propelled artillery battalions. The 1942 Armored Division fielded 14,620 men, 390 tanks and almost 800 half-tracks (3,500 vehicles of all types). This type of formation was soon termed a 'heavy division'. For manoeuvre operations in the field the units of the division were divided between Combat Commands A and B (CCA and CCB). The combat commands were essentially task forces configured as required for their mission and able to operate independently.

By 1943 the 1st, 2nd, and 3rd Armored Divisions (heavy) were considered too unwieldy. All the later-formed divisions dispensed with the regimental level of command. They were organised into three tank battalions, three armoured infantry battalions, three artillery battalions and a reconnaissance squadron. These new 'light' armoured divisions had 10,900 men and 260 tanks. In combat the battalions were to be divided between CCA, CCB and the new Combat Command

North Africa, January 1943: the crew of a 1st Armored Division M3 Medium tank (Grant) unpack 75mm shells from their black cardboard shipping tubes. Most wear HBT overalls with a mixture of 'M1941' Parsons field jackets and cold weather 'tanker' jackets. The three men at the left wear the light khaki padded fabric 'winter combat helmet' which was designed to fit under the hardened leather 'armored forces helmet', worn here by the third man from the right. By the end of the Tunisian campaign M4 Shermans had replaced most M3s in US Army tank units.

1943 (Light) Armored Division

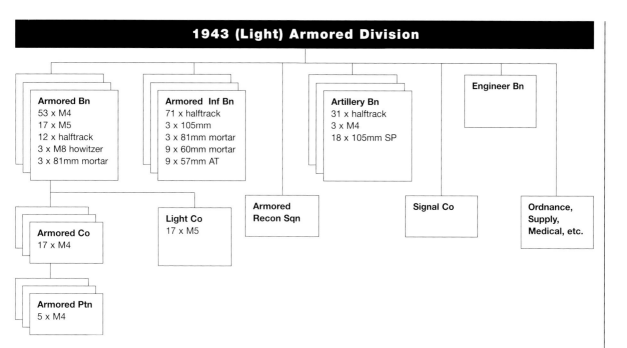

Armored Bn
53 x M4
17 x M5
12 x halftrack
3 x M8 howitzer
3 x 81mm mortar

Armored Inf Bn
71 x halftrack
3 x 105mm
3 x 81mm mortar
9 x 60mm mortar
9 x 57mm AT

Artillery Bn
31 x halftrack
3 x M4
18 x 105mm SP

Engineer Bn

Light Co
17 x M5

Armored Recon Sqn

Signal Co

Ordnance, Supply, Medical, etc.

Armored Co
17 x M4

Armored Ptn
5 x M4

Reserve (CCR). The 1st Armored Division shifted to the new light configuration in July 1944, but the 2nd and 3rd retained their heavy organisation throughout the war. It was the fully mechanised US armoured divisions of 1944 with their radios, self-propelled artillery and air-liaison teams which truly executed the *blitzkrieg* as envisioned by the Germans at the outbreak of the war.

A US Army tank battalion consisted of about 71 tanks and 729 men organised into three tank companies (by 1943/44, with M4 Shermans), a light tank company (M5 Stuarts), and HQ and Service Companies. The battalion, commanded by a lieutenant-colonel, also included three 81mm mortars and three tank-mounted M8 snub-nosed 75mm howitzers. Each tank company had three platoons of five tanks each and a HQ of two tanks. A howitzer tank was added to each company in the last year of the war.

Besides the tank battalions assigned to armoured divisions, independent General Headquarters (GHQ) tank battalions were available for assignment by armies to corps and divisions as necessary (in 1944, about 65, with another 29 in process of formation). As infantry divisions were without integral tank units, it was common in Europe to

August 1944: 'glider riders' of the 1st Airborne Task Force emerge from their Waco CG-4A near La Motte, South of France, after what appears to have been a lucky landing. All are armed with carbines. The Waco carried 13 men, or four men and a jeep.

assign independent tank and tank destroyer battalions to such divisions for extended periods.

Airborne Divisions

As with the Armored Force, it took the sharp example of the German paratroops in 1940–41 to get the US Airborne off the ground. An airborne training battalion (501st) was rapidly expanded into a regiment; and soon the 82nd Infantry Division found itself converting to the airborne role. Men of the 82nd then provided cadres for the 101st Airborne as it formed. The 82nd fought in Sicily and Italy, then in North-West Europe; the 101st made their first assault alongside the 82nd on D-Day, and fought in North-West Europe until VE-Day. The 11th, 13th and 17th Airborne Divisions followed. The 11th went to the Pacific; the 17th saw combat in the Battle of the Bulge and in Germany; the 13th made it to Europe in 1945, but did not see combat. An African-American parachute battalion (555th) was raised, but never left the United States.

Paratroopers – all volunteers – had to complete rigorous physical training and five jumps before they were awarded their 'jump wings'. With their trousers smartly tucked into their cherished Corcoran jump boots, the Parachute Infantry Regiment (PIR) troopers referred to all non-paratroop GIs as 'straight legs'. The 'glider riders' of Glider Infantry

OPPOSITE **North Africa, November 1942: men of the 1st Rangers check a French fort. Note their shortened web leggings, left shoulder flag patches, and white recognition armbands. The right hand man has an unofficial open-top holster.**

OPPOSITE, BELOW **Col. William O. Darby, 1st Rangers, on his personal Harley-Davidson; note his favoured 03 Springfield rifle in the leather scabbard.**

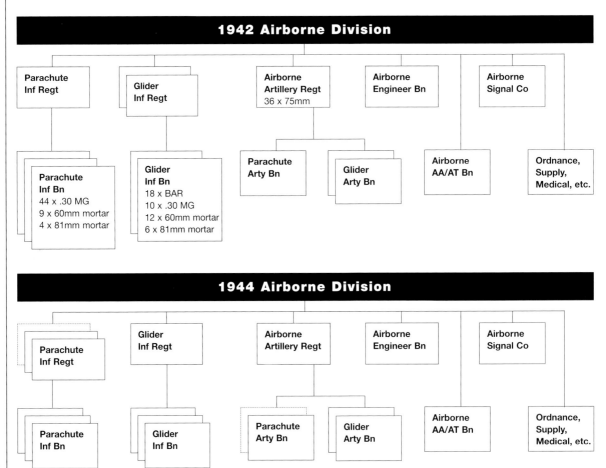

1942 Airborne Division

- Parachute Inf Regt
  - Parachute Inf Bn
    44 x .30 MG
    9 x 60mm mortar
    4 x 81mm mortar
- Glider Inf Regt
  - Glider Inf Bn
    18 x BAR
    10 x .30 MG
    12 x 60mm mortar
    6 x 81mm mortar
- Airborne Artillery Regt
  36 x 75mm
  - Parachute Arty Bn
  - Glider Arty Bn
- Airborne Engineer Bn
  - Airborne AA/AT Bn
- Airborne Signal Co
  - Ordnance, Supply, Medical, etc.

1944 Airborne Division

- Parachute Inf Regt
  - Parachute Inf Bn
- Glider Inf Regt
  - Glider Inf Bn
- Airborne Artillery Regt
  - Parachute Arty Bn
  - Glider Arty Bn
- Airborne Engineer Bn
  - Airborne AA/AT Bn
- Airborne Signal Co
  - Ordnance, Supply, Medical, etc.

Regiments (GIR) were commonly 'leg' infantry units who were simply assigned to the Airborne. A quarter of the 82nd Division went over the fence for a few days when first told of their new status. For the dubious pleasure of riding a crash-landing glider into combat they initially received no distinctions or extra pay (a special glider badge and hazardous duty pay were belatedly awarded in 1945). The Waco CG-4A glider they rode was possibly piloted by a washed-out Air Corps pilot (warrant officer), and was likely to break apart on landing. It was not comforting to know that some of the Wacos were built by a coffin manufacturer. While test riding a glider the city council of St Louis were all killed when the wing of their Waco broke off. The Waco was probably the best glider of the war, but it was inevitably fragile. When a Nisei GI riding one into the invasion of the South of France poked a small hole in one to see out, he spent the rest of the trip holding the hole closed so that the whole side of the glider did not rip off.

The original airborne divisions were small; the 1942 division called for 8,400 men in one parachute and two glider infantry regiments, with a single three-battalion Airborne Artillery Regiment divided between the two roles. The GIRs totalled 1,600 men in two battalions and the PIRs had 1,000 men in three battalions. The 11th Airborne Division, which served in the Pacific, retained this organisation but retrained most of their glider men for the parachute role, partly due to a shortage of gliders in theatre. Airborne artillery consisted of three (later four) battalions of glider/parachute pack 75/105mm howitzers. By 1943 the divisional establishment had changed to one glider and two parachute regiments with both units increased in size. The actual organisation and strength of each Airborne formation varied with time and mission, and there was a lot of cross-posting (see Elite 31, *US Army Airborne 1940–90* for details). The 82nd had three regiments in the Mediterranean but left one behind (504th) when it deployed to England in 1944; the 504th PIR fought at Anzio. The 82nd's Normandy airdrop was made with one glider and three parachute regiments, but the 504th, which had rejoined the division by now, was left behind in England. By December 1944 during the Battle of the Bulge a larger 13,000-man airborne divisional establishment was authorised to catch up with the already expanded 82nd and 101st Divisions.

Airborne units were small and lightly equipped. Regardless of the outstanding quality of their troopers, they had trouble sustaining themselves in combat due to their inherent lack of vehicles, artillery and men. It was wasteful to keep them in combat as conventional infantry for long after their assault landings, but this was often required by the exigencies of battle. The Salerno operation became so desperate that part of the 82nd were airdropped into the beachhead to provide direct reinforcement. In order for the airborne divisions to stay in combat they had to be augmented with additional support and combat units.

Ranger Battalions

Impressed by the elan and effectiveness of the British Commandos, the US Army authorised the founding of a similar battalion of specially trained GIs. In June 1942, 500 volunteers from the 34th and 1st Armored Divisions in Northern Ireland were formed into the 1st Ranger Battalion, named for the old Colonial ranger companies of the French and Indian War; they were commanded by a 34th Division artillery major, William O.Darby. These men were run through the demanding British Commando training school in Scotland. The success of the 1st Rangers in spearheading part of the landings in Vichy North Africa and actions in Tunisia encouraged the formation of further battalions.

The 2nd Ranger Bn was formed in the USA in April 1943 and saw its first action at Omaha Beach and Pointe du Hoc on D-Day. The 3rd and 4th Rangers were formed in North Africa around cadres from the 1st Bn, and made the Sicily landing in July 1943. The 5th Bn was formed in the USA in September 1943 and underwent Commando training in England; they first saw action on Omaha Beach. The 6th Rangers were formed in the Pacific in August 1944 and fought in the 1944/45 liberation of the Philippines.

Ranger battalions were small, having only 26 officers and 354 enlisted men. They usually comprised one HQ company and six Ranger companies, the latter with three officers and 59 EMs; each company had two platoons, usually consisting of two assault sections and a special weapons section. By 1944 the battalion's heavy weapons scale included 6 x 81mm mortars, 18 x 60mm mortars, 14 x 2.36in bazookas, and 24 x .30cal MGs (often replaced by BARs). In North Africa, D Company, 1st Rangers had the 81mm mortars, but this was soon changed and the mortars were spread among the companies. The three-battalion Ranger Force that went into Sicily had a 4.2in mortar battalion attached. By the time of the Italy landings the Ranger Force had added a four-gun 105mm halftrack Cannon Company.

The Rangers made excellent spearhead troops and would participate in every amphibious landing in Europe except the South of France, where their place was taken by the 1st SSF – see below. (For unit details see Elite 13, *US Army Rangers & LRRP Units 1942–87*.) Like the paratroopers, however, the Rangers were often misused as regular infantry by field commanders. The problem with Ranger units was that they were generally too big for Commando raids and too small and unsupported for conventional operations. In a famous incident at Anzio the 1st and 3rd Bns were wiped out in a ferocious one-day tank and infantry battle. Due to severe losses at Anzio the 4th Rangers were

PAYSCALE

Soldiers' pay was calculated based on their pay grade, the senior NCOs being 'grade 1'; after the war the grades were reversed, i.e. the first sergeant/master sergeant became 'grade 8' (E8). Those holding technician rank received slightly more than base pay for their grade. GIs were paid an extra $5 a month if they qualified as a firing expert, $5 for the Expert Infantryman Badge and $10 for the Combat Infantryman Badge. Paratroopers received an extra $50 a month 'hazardous duty pay'. Time in grade also boosted pay. Before September 1942 the first sergeant was grade 2 with three stripes, a diamond and two rockers. Pay in Europe was usually in local currency. Base pay by late 1942 was as follows:

Private	(recruit)	$21
Private	(7th grade)	$30
Pfc	(6th grade)	$36
Corporal	(5th grade)	$54
Sergeant	(4th grade)	$60
Staff Sgt	(3rd grade)	$72
Technical Sgt	(2nd grade)	$84
1Sgt/MSgt	(1st grade)	$126
2Lt/WO		$150

disbanded; some of these orphaned Rangers were transferred into the 1st SSF, where they wore both the Force's arrowhead patch and the Ranger scroll. Colonel Darby was killed in action as a TF commander in the 10th Mountain Division a week before VE-Day.

10th Mountain Division

Experimenting with lightly equipped divisions, and impressed by European mountain troops, the US Army decided that it too needed a mountain division. The 10th Mountain Division was recruited primarily from among outdoorsmen from the western states, who were trained in skiing and mountaineering in the Colorado Rocky Mountains. Their special clothing issue is outlined earlier in this text. The 14,100-man division had three infantry regiments (85th, 86th and 87th), as well as 6,000 horses and mules, and some M29 Weasel tracked snow vehicles in lieu of trucks. The divisional artillery comprised 36 pack howitzers. Refused by the high command in the ETO, this promising division arrived in Italy in January 1945, and proved perfectly suited for combat in the Italian Alps.

1st Special Service Force

On 20 July 1942 former coastal artillery Col Robert T.Frederick was given a free hand to create a brigade-sized unit for a Churchill-inspired mission into occupied Norway. Uniquely, this was a bi-national force: 30-40% of his unit were crack Canadian volunteers. The GIs were mostly volunteers who responded to Frederick's call for 'paratroops, ski troops and commandos'. Some were 'discipline problems' from units that took

Anzio beachhead, January 1944: this Canadian Forceman of the FSSF wears the second pattern reversible parka white side out. Note also the two-part cloth/wool mittens; and the M1941 Johnson light machine gun, a weapon peculiar to the Force – 125 were acquired before leaving the USA by bartering two tons of plastic explosive with the US Marines.

South of France, August 1944: British paras and GIs of the 1st Airborne Task Force take a break. Note the national flag armbands and patches, respectively. The left hand GI seems to have camouflage-painted his uniform (see Plate F1) and has padding under his web suspenders.

the traditional opportunity to shift their problems elsewhere, but all had to be personally approved by Col Frederick, who was looking for aggressive and intelligent outdoorsmen for his intended Commando-style unit. They were highly trained in hand-to-hand combat, demolitions, speed marching, winter and alpine operations, airborne and amphibious warfare. Innocuously named the 1st Special Service Force (FSSF), the unit had 1,800 men broken into three 'regiments' and a 500-man support unit; GIs and Canadians were mixed together throughout.

Their first action was not in Norway but in the Aleutians in August 1943, but the Japanese were found to have already pulled out of Kiska. The Force was then sent to Italy in November 1943, with an attached airborne artillery battalion. In the Anzio beachhead and in the mountains they proved themselves as elite infantry. At Anzio a German diary said of the Forcemen 'The Black Devils are all around us every time we come into the line, and we never hear them come'. In the South of France they seized in Commando style an empty coastal artillery battery; and served out the remainder of their war with Gen Frederick's new command, the 1st Airborne Task Force. Also known as 'the Devil's Brigade' or simply 'the North Americans', the FSSF was disbanded in December 1944.

1st Airborne Task Force

The planned invasion of the South of France in August 1944 called for an airborne element, but no airborne division was available in the

Eastern France, November 1944: command post (CP) of Co.F, 442nd Regimental Combat Team. The white lieutenant (right, wearing mackinaw) is probably the company commander; behind him is his radio operator with an SCR 300. The four Nisei GIs all wear the M1943 field jacket. The regiment earned much praise for its behaviour during the savage winter fighting in the Belfort Gap.

Mediterranean theatre. A patched-together 1st Airborne Task Force (1st ATF) was therefore created, commanded by Gen Frederick of the FSSF. Near Rome, Frederick gathered up all the independent airborne units in theatre and set up a jump training school at a nearby airfield. In the main the 1st ATF consisted of the following Parachute Infantry units: 509th Bn, 517th Regt, 1Bn/551st Regt, 550th Bn, and the British 2nd Independent Parachute Bde (4, 5 and 6 Battalions). They were supported by the 460th, 463rd and 602nd Airborne Field Artillery Bns; and a glider-borne anti-tank gun company of the 442nd (Nisei) Regiment. The formation totalled about 10,000 men.

The 1st ATF was short of jump boots, and at least one unit set out to solve this problem in an unorthodox manner. A group of them went on pass into Rome, and proceeded to mug for their boots any rear area GIs and MPs they found wearing the unauthorised paratroop footwear.

Just as in Sicily, the South of France drop was widely scattered; but Frederick's men seized all their objectives and raised hell in the German rear areas, including the capture of a corps headquarters. Amazingly, Frederick's ersatz division remained in combat (the British brigade having been replaced by the FSSF) until November 1944, with no transport or logistics support. They became expert at purloining vehicles and rerouting supplies to maintain themselves in combat. The ATF was finally broken up in November and its men assigned to the 101st and 82nd Airborne Divisions (XVIII Airborne Corps).

Ethnic units: the Nisei

The 100th Battalion, 1,500 strong, was formed mainly from Hawaiian National Guardsmen of Japanese-American descent (Nisei). These troops were rerun through basic and unit training and were eventually forwarded to Europe. They were deployed to Italy in September 1943 as a part of the 34th Division. In the meantime, the 442nd Regimental Combat Team was formed from Nisei in Hawaii and the 'relocation' camps in the USA; it consisted of three rifle battalions and an artillery battalion (552nd), with a mixture of white and Nisei officers. With part of one battalion left behind, the 442nd joined the 34th Division and the 100th Bn just after the Anzio breakout in July 1944. In September the 442nd RCT, now incorporating the 100th Bn, was redeployed to the South of France and attached to the 36th 'Texas' Division. In support of the 36th, the Niseis' most famous combat action occurred near Belmont. After two vicious days of fighting, the 442nd came to the rescue of a surrounded battalion of grateful Texans. Leaving the artillery battalion behind to serve in Germany, the 442nd RCT was reassigned to the 34th Division in Italy. It finished the war as part of the reconstituted 92nd Division. The 442nd RCT was the most highly decorated regiment of the US Army; the 100th Bn alone won three Distinguished Unit Citations.

It is worth noting that not all Nisei soldiers served in the 442nd RCT; a handful of them served in other ETO units, and a few in the Pacific as translators/interrogators.

African-American troops

Although all-black units (officered primarily by whites) had been a part of the US Army since the Civil War, even in World War II it was still generally felt (though it is hard to imagine on what supposed

Italy, 1943: a shirtsleeved Nisei GI of the 100th Bn – judging from his just-visible binocular case, an NCO – photographed while commanding a 60mm mortar crew of his company's heavy weapons platoon. Note the 'Red Bull' shoulder patch of the 34th Division; the 100th replaced the 2/133rd Infantry in this division, and distinguished itself during the Cassino fighting of winter 1943/44 (see Plate D2).

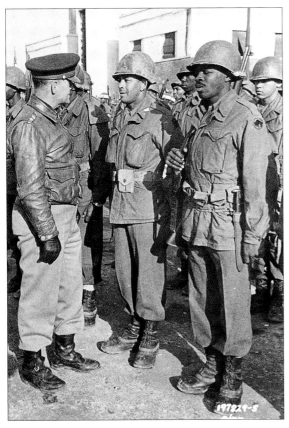

historical evidence) that blacks would make poor combat soldiers. As a result, most of the African-American GIs initially served in rear area Quartermaster, Engineer, Signal and Transport units. Indeed, 60% of the famous 'Red Ball Express' were black. Manpower shortages and pressure from the Army Chief of Staff saw about 5% of the black GIs organised into two divisions (92nd and 93rd) and over 30 independent artillery and tank units.

Hopes were high that these units would perform well. Unfortunately, many of the unhappy white officers assigned to black units were (intentionally) Southerners, and had low expectations of their troops. After an uncertain start the 93rd Division in the Pacific performed outstanding, though limited, combat service.

The independent battalions also did well, the 969th Artillery and 761st Tank Battalions being among the most notable. The 92nd Division, however, fared poorly. Badly trained and badly led, its service in northern Italy in 1945 was at best uninspiring. Its original infantry units were the 365th, 370th and 371st Regiments; it was finally reorganised to have one white, one black, and one Nisei (the 442nd) infantry regiments.

Although the Army still refused formal integration, the dire need for infantry replacements encouraged Gen Eisenhower to call for black GIs in support units to volunteer for combat duty in the ETO. Some 10,000 blacks – including NCOs who agreed to accept reduction to private – were forwarded to white units as squad- and platoon- sized reinforcements. The results were generally good; and the Army moved another step closer to full integration.

Northern Italy, December 1944: Gen Truscott, commanding 5th Army, inspects troops of the African-American 92nd Division; note the 'buffalo' shoulder patch at right. Truscott wears a leather flyer's jacket and private purchase strapped boots; the GIs wear the M1943 jacket with wool trousers and M1944 'shoepacs'.

CREW-SERVED WEAPONS

Machine guns

The Browning M1917 water-cooled machine gun was introduced to the US Army in the trenches of 1918. Arguably the best machine gun of the Great War, this solid and reliable weapon would provide the basis of all the machine guns used by GIs in World War II. The M1917s on hand (70,000) were slightly modified to the M1917A1 configuration just prior to 1941. During the war some 55,000 additional M1917A1s were produced by Rock Island, Colt and Brown-LC. Wartime modifications included the replacement of some bronze components with steel, and the bolt was improved.

The M1917A1 was a water-cooled .30 calibre belt-fed heavy machine gun; gun and tripod weighed 93lbs (42kg) 'wet' (41 & 52lbs respectively). Its rate of fire was 500-600 rounds per minute (rpm). It excelled in sustained fire work in defence and perimeter coverage, but was found to be too heavy for rapid moves forward in the attack. The

M1917A1 was usually to be seen in the Heavy Weapons Companies and was sometimes mounted on half-tracks. Due to its weight some Heavy Weapons units discarded it in favour of the lighter air-cooled M1919A4.

At the end of World War I an air-cooled M1919 machine gun for tank and air use was developed by modifying the M1917 (removing the water jacket). In the 1930s various improvements were made for its use by the infantry, with the final version designated the M1919A4. About 389,000 M1919A4s were made by Colt, Saginaw and Buffalo during the war. This gun, and the M2 cavalry tripod which was found best for general issue, totalled 45lbs (20.4kg) and had a heavier barrel with a slim ventilated metal cooling jacket, with a 500rpm rate of fire. The A4 was almost universally used at infantry platoon level and in tanks. It was also found that a BAR bipod could be mounted for rough terrain and light machine gun use. A wheeled cart was available to transport machine guns but it was not commonly seen.

Near Naples, September 1943: a weapons company man from the 36th Division mans his M1917A1 machine gun. He wears the M1928 pack, and a pick-mattock slung on his hip; his helmet chinstrap is hooked up to the netting. In the background is a British Sherman tank of the Royal Scots Greys.

The even lighter M1919A6 machine gun came into issue in 1944. Based on the A4, the A6 had a detachable shoulder stock, folding bipod, carrying handle and lighter barrel, the entire assembly weighing 32lbs. It was issued throughout the Army but was especially noticeable in the Airborne units. The A6 was newly manufactured by Saginaw (43,000), though many were modified A4s.

Both the M1919A4 and A6 were capable of being used on the move, awkwardly fired from the hip, though a heavily gloved hand holding the barrel or a temporary sling was required. This unhappy kind of compromise was not recommended for accuracy or good health. The 250-round ammo belt was usually cut short for this operation.

Italy, October 1944: machine gunner firing the M1919A6 with shoulder stock; the white canvas belts are very visible here, as they were on the battlefield.

GIs were generally happy with the powerful and reliable M1919 series; their biggest complaint, however, arose when they compared it to the German MG34/42 series. The MG42 especially was lighter (25lbs); it was easier for the crew to change hot barrels; and it had a significantly higher and intimidating rate of fire (1,100rpm). Regardless of Ordnance opinions about balancing accuracy and ammo conservation, it was still felt that German machine guns had an edge. GIs also disliked the white cloth ammo belts, as the cloth would sometimes catch in the mechanism. The belts finally came in OD in the last year of the war, as did the new disintegrating metal link belts still in use today. The A6 could handle the new metal links, but the A4 had problems. Good machine gunners took time over cleaning and reseating the rounds in the belt.

The machine gun squad consisted of the gun and five men: a gunner and assistant gunner who fired and fed in the ammo, and two ammo

bearers, all under command of a 'buck sergeant' or corporal squad leader.

The .50 calibre machine gun was created in 1919 as an anti-tank/aircraft weapon based on the M1917 and the World War I German anti-tank rifle. The Army and Navy eventually bought about 1,000 water-cooled M1921 .50cal guns, mainly for anti-aircraft use. In the 1930s a version was created with a longer, heavier, air-cooled barrel for vehicle and ground use, and designated the M2HB. The gun weighed 81lbs (36.7kg) and the M3 tripod another 44lbs (20kg). Its cyclic rate was about 450rpm; the 'big fifty' fired ball, AP, tracer and incendiary, and could be belt fed with metal link from either side. A water-cooled M2 weighing 121lbs 'wet' was also made for anti-aircraft use. Some 347,000 M2s were made during the war for ground use by seven different manufacturers including AC Sparkplug and Frigidaire. One .50cal could be found in the heavy weapons platoon of the infantry rifle company, and they were also mounted on any number of vehicles from tanks to trucks and jeeps, though in the latter case the strain of firing was very hard on the light vehicle frame. The four-barrelled 'quad-fifty' mounted on a halftrack or trailer for anti-aircraft use could also destroy almost any ground target except heavy armour, and was nick-named 'the meat chopper'. Even a single .50cal firing from a foxhole could be guaranteed to put an entire German infantry company on its face. The impact of the 700-grain slug on a human body can only be imagined. This classic weapon is still in use world-wide.

Bazookas

Before the war the Army Ordnance Dept – like their Napoleonic predecessors – had played around with rockets of various sizes, considering their practicality as weapons of war. By 1942 they had developed a tubular shoulder-fired rocket launcher, but were unsure what warhead to mount for what purpose. As the Army was scrambling for anti-tank weapons, an M10 AT grenade was fixed onto the front of the rocket. It was immediately recognised as the perfect infantryman's AT weapon. Informally named the 'bazooka' after a comic's fanciful musical instrument, it was rushed into production; General Electric got a 30-day

North Africa, June 1943: a bazooka team from the 505th PIR, 82nd Airborne Division, use mortar shell vests to carry extra 2.36in rocket rounds. The No.2's job was to load the rocket and attach its firing wire to the terminal on the tube; he then slapped the No.1's helmet, and got well clear of the backblast. Note the early T-handle shovels, and the No.1's M1A1 folding stock carbine, skein of rope and apparently custom-made ammo pouches 'rigger'.

contract to deliver 5,000 of them. Half that time was spent creating an acceptable prototype. The bazookas were delivered to the ports with 90 minutes to spare on the contract. Literally fresh from the factory, the bazookas were handed out to somewhat bewildered GIs aboard ships bound for the North African landings of November 1942.

The bazooka was a 4.5ft-long steel tube weighing 18lbs (8.1kg). It fired a 2.36in rocket warhead, as that was the size of the M10 shaped charge AT grenade. The first model (M1) had two firing handles and crude sights, and used a flashlight battery in the wooden stock to ignite the rocket. A two-man firer and loader team operated the weapon. The bazooka was used in Tunisia, and although it is doubtful if it destroyed a single enemy tank it gave the GIs something to fight back with. The forward handhold was found to be unnecessary; and in hot weather the rocket motors sometimes detonated in the tube.

The improved M1A had wire tightly wrapped around the back half of the tube for strength and the forward handle was eliminated. By late 1943 the new M9A1 bazooka was in production. This could be broken down for carriage in two halves (16lbs) and its trigger-operated magneto replaced the battery. The rocket and warhead were also improved. The backblast of the rocket motor proved a troublesome problem for the operators. Goggles and special facemasks were issued, but most GIs did not bother. A round muzzle shield was also used, but it was fragile and commonly disappeared. Though underpowered by 1944/45 standards, the 2.36in bazooka proved a godsend to the infantryman exposed to enemy armoured attacks. It could keep tanks at arm's length, and with a lucky hit it could knock them out or immobilise them. Interestingly, the British declined the bazooka, but the Russians received and used a shipment of them in 1942. It is probably from this source that the Germans captured one, and later copied it to produce their 88mm Panzershreck.

When used aggressively against enemy armour unprotected by infantry, tank-hunting teams could do real damage. GIs in both the Pacific and Europe also found the bazooka excellent for busting walls and bunkers. Pfc Carl V. Sheridan of the 47th Infantry (9th ID) was awarded a posthumous Medal of Honor for his attack on Frenzenberg Castle with a bazooka. With his stovepipe and ammo picked up from a wounded bearer, he joined his company in a furious fight with about 70 enemy paratroopers in the castle courtyard:

'... With complete disregard for his own safety (he) left the protection of the buildings and in the face of heavy and intense small arms and grenade fire, crossed the courtyard to the drawbridge entrance where he could bring direct fire to bear against the (oak) door. Although handicapped by the lack of an assistant, and a constant target for the enemy fire that burst around him, he skillfully and effectively handled

Italy, 1944: a brigadier-general and a captain (S2 – intelligence officer) of the 1st Armored Division examine a captured 88mm *Raketen Panzerbuchse 54* ('*Panzerschreck*'), the German anti-tank weapon copied from US bazookas captured on the Russian Front. Note that both wear the divisional patch on their left chest instead of the shoulder (see Plate E2).

Near Colmar, France, December 1944: a 4.2in mortar crew of the 83rd Chemical Bn in action. This unit had supported the Ranger Force in the Sicily landings.

his awkward weapon to place two well aimed rockets into the structure. Observing that the door was only weakened, and realizing a gap must be made for a successful assault, he loaded his last rocket, took careful aim, and blasted a hole through the heavy planks. Turning to his company, he shouted "Come on, let's get them!" With his pistol blazing, he charged into the gaping entrance and was killed by the withering fire that met him. The final assault on the castle was made through the gap which Pfc Sheridan gave his life to create.'

Recoilless rifles

By mid-1943 the Army was testing 'recoilless rifles' (RCL) for anti-tank and general use. This weapon vented the majority of its propellant gases out the rear of the breech, making it virtually recoilless. It was normally fired from the shoulder like a bazooka, or from a M1917 machine gun tripod mount; it was slightly longer than a bazooka and weighed 45lbs (20.4kg). The RCL could fire HE, anti-tank or smoke rounds. First fielded in 1945 in Europe, the initial M18 57mm version proved very effective and its range, accuracy and hitting power made it popular among GI users. The M20 75mm recoilless also made it to the front in 1945; its 115lb weight (52kg) and almost seven feet in length forced the use of the M1917 mount. Both the 57mm and 75mm were found to be excellent for airborne use. Though available in very limited numbers in both Europe and Okinawa, the RCLs gave infantrymen an excellent bunker-buster and anti-tank weapon.

Mortars

Veteran Bill Mauldin summed up mortars thus: 'Outside of the bazooka, they carry more viciousness and wallop per pound than any weapon the infantry has.' An infantry regiment would have at least 27 x 60mm and 18 x 81mm tubes; three 60s served in the weapons platoon of each rifle company and six 81s in the battalion's heavy weapons company. Perhaps the biggest virtue of these weapons was that they were owned and operated by the frontline infantry themselves. Because they were so far forward they made tempting targets, however; and, like the machine guns, they never seemed to have enough ammunition.

Mortars operate by dropping the 'bomb' or shell down the tube; a shotgun shell primer in the base hits the stud in the bottom of the mortar tube, which ignites the small bags of powder which propel the shell out. The range and accuracy are determined by the elevation of the barrel and the number of propellant packets left on the shell by the crew.

The US M2 60mm mortar was developed in 1939 and was essentially a down-scaled 81mm. The weapon weighed 42lbs (19kg) and could fire HE, smoke, and illumination (parachute flares). The 3lb (1.36kg) HE shell had a maximum range of 2,000 yards.

The US M1 81mm mortar was basically a 1930s French improvement on the British World War I Stokes mortar. It could fire HE, smoke, white phosphorus and illumination, the shells varying in weight from 7lbs to

15lbs (11kg–24kg) each. Like the 60mm, this 135lb (61kg) weapon could be broken into three parts for carrying. The M43A1 (7lb) light HE shell had a range of 3,290 yards. In mechanised units particularly, 81mm mortars were sometimes mounted on halftracks.

The 4.2in (106mm) chemical mortar was developed after World War I by the Chemical Corps to project gas and smoke shells. Unlike the smoot-bore 60mm and 81mm, this was a rifled mortar, and improved M1A1 and M2 versions were the most common 4.2s in use. Its weight of 330lbs (149.6kg) made it transportable by vehicle or mule only. The development of HE rounds for the chemical 'four-deuce' made it a formidable weapon, firing smoke, HE, WP and chemical shells over 3,000 yards. These weapons were formed into Chemical Corps-operated 4.2in mortar battalions, and used as corps level assets for assignment as needed. One of their first employments was in Sicily in support of the Ranger battalions. (The Army also developed a 155mm mortar, a few of which were used in the 1945 campaign for the Philippines.)

VEHICLES

'Soft skin vehicles'

Although interested readers should pursue this very large subject in other relevant books, a few words on the most widely used vehicles may be helpful.

After some minor experimentation with half-ton 4x4 trucks, the Army called for manufacturers to produce a light 1,300lb (590kg) truck for testing in 1940. Bantam, Willys and Ford produced models, with the over-weight (2,160lb) Willys model deemed the winner. During the war both Willys and Ford would produce 650,000 of these four-cylinder wonders. Its 60 horsepower engine could propel the vehicle up steep inclines and through mud as well as reaching 55mph on roads. If it got stuck, it was small and light enough to be lifted out of trouble by several GIs or any other vehicle. It was called either a Peep or a Jeep (after the cartoon character Sweetpea's pet creature). The jeep could carry three to four men, had a payload of 800lbs (362kg) and could haul a trailer. It was in heavy demand by all the Allies, and even the Germans loved driving captured jeeps. It could be armed with a .30cal machine gun, and .50s were sometimes (precariously) substituted. A vertical bar was often welded to the front of the vehicle to cut wires strung neck-high across roads.

Also purchased in significant numbers was the Harley Davidson motorcycle. Some 60,000

Italy, January 1944: 34th Division artillery forward observers (FOs) plan a strike from the back of their jeep. The snow chains on the tyres were commonly retained for traction in mud.

WLA model Harleys, whose design was somewhat influenced by German cycles, became Army property. The Harley weighed 512lbs (233kg) and was driven by a 23hp engine. They were heavily used by the Military Police and couriers, and a leather rifle scabbard was commonly attached to the right front.

During the war Dodge produced 82,000 utility ¾-ton 4x4 trucks for the Army. Sometimes known as a 'weapons carrier', this truck had a six-cylinder engine and a 1,500lb (680kg) payload. They could be found throughout the Army hauling both men and equipment, and an unsuccessful early version (M6) mounted the 37mm anti-tank gun. A Dodge 'command car' and a 6x6 truck version were also produced, as was the 4x4 ambulance. Each medical battalion had about 33 ambulances which could hold four stretcher cases each.

The GMC 2½-ton 6x6 truck was a commercially available vehicle in 1940. With a 9,200lb (4173kg) payload, the 'deuce and a half' or 'Jimmy' was made in more than 800,000 examples by GMC, Studebaker, International and Reo. For a cargo truck this powerful vehicle had excellent cross-country ability. The Jimmy was the main cargo vehicle

Tunisia, March 1943: MPs from the 1st Armored Division see off a 'Jimmy-load' of German POWs. The MP at right seems to have a (rare) yellow or white brassard, and the divisional sign painted on his helmet front. The holster of the MP at left can be seen, under magnification, to be decorated with Italian eagle and star insignia and a German wound badge.

France, 1944: M2 halftrack from an Armored Division mounting an 81mm mortar; and note at left the 'roller coaster' rail for mounting machine guns. This is a good example of the 'gypsy caravan' look which US vehicles tended to acquire during a campaign of movement.

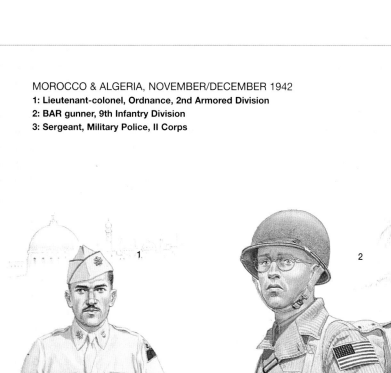

MOROCCO & ALGERIA, NOVEMBER/DECEMBER 1942

1: Lieutenant-colonel, Ordnance, 2nd Armored Division

2: BAR gunner, 9th Infantry Division

3: Sergeant, Military Police, II Corps

A

TUNISIA, WINTER 1942/SPRING 1943
1: Sergeant, bazooka gunner, 1st Infantry Division
2: Infantry private, 1st Infantry Division
3: Sergeant of a tank unit, 1st Armored Division

1

2

3

B

SICILY, SUMMER 1943
1: Machine gun crewman, 3rd Infantry Division
2: Corporal, machine gunner, 3rd Infantry Division
3: Private first class, 3rd Ranger Battalion

C

ITALY, 1943/44
1: 1st Lt, Field Artillery, 36th Infantry Division
2: Technician 4th grade, 100th Battalion
3: S/Sgt, Field Artillery, 34th Infantry Division

D

ANZIO, JANUARY 1944
1: Medical orderly, VI Corps
2: Major of a tank unit, 1st Armored Division
3: Pfc, 1st Special Service Force

E

SOUTH & EAST FRANCE, 1944
1: Capt, 1/551st PIR, 1st Airborne Task Force
2: Brigadier-general, US Army
3: Pfc, infantry, 45th Infantry Division

F

ITALY, 1945
1: Staff captain, HQ 5th Army
2: Master sergeant, 10th Mountain Division
3: Infantry private, 10th Mountain Division

G

PO VALLEY, 1945
1: 1st Lt, 701st Tank Destroyer Battalion
2: Infantry sergeant, 92nd Infantry Division
3: 2nd Lt, 92nd Infantry Division

used at divisional level. It could be modified to serve many specialised purposes: hauling fuel, people, or any kind of supplies; as a tow truck, or – with a built-up box back – as a workshop. Heavier trucks like the 4x2, 4x4, 6x4, and 6x6 were also produced, the '6x's being commonly used in the Red/White Ball Express priority convoy system.

By 1944 the two-ton M29 Weasel was to be seen with the 10th Mountain Division (it was originally intended for the FSSF's raid into Norway). A small, broad-tracked amphibian shaped like a bathtub, it was specially modified to cross snow, at which it excelled. The Weasel had a Studebaker 65hp engine which gave it speeds of 3 to 4mph on water and 36mph (58k/ph) on land. It could carry three passengers or 1,200lbs (545kg) of cargo.

Italy, December 1943: in the mountains, packhorses and mules were a great deal more practical than vehicles, and fulfilled a high proportion of the Allies' front line logisitic needs. Here troopers of the 504th Parachute Infantry load up a donkey with a M1919A4 machine gun. Note that the man at right has a World War I canteen and a bolt-action 03 Springfield rifle; and note the snap-fastened cargo pocket marking him as Airborne.

Halftracks

The ubiquitous halftrack series was initially a replacement for the M3A1 four-wheeled scout car, whose Hercules 87hp engine was underpowered for cross-country use, though it could reach a top road speed of 50mph (80k/ph). The open-topped M3A1 was armed with a .30cal and a .50cal MG on skate mountings riding a 'roller-coaster' track which allowed the weapons all-round fire. Almost 21,000 were produced by White in 1939–44. They could carry six men in the rear, protected (from small arms fire only) by half-inch armour. A few scout cars and 46 halftracks were in the Philippines by November 1941.

By 1940 the artillery were looking for a hybrid halftracked prime mover, and the infantry were also interested in a halftrack personnel carrier which could keep up with the tanks across country. The M3 and slightly shorter M2 halftracks began issue in 1941. The M2/M3 had a 147hp gas engine with a top speed of 45mph (72k/ph). Both the steerable front wheels and the rear tracks were powered. The front bumper commonly mounted a winch or a large roller for getting over obstacles.

The M2 rear compartment was one foot shorter than the M3 and, like the scout car, it had an all-round MG mounting track and no rear door; it held seven men, and had interior storage bins. The M2 was commonly used as a prime mover for the artillery. The M3 was intended for infantry use and could seat ten men in the rear, with a rear hull door. It was armed with a .30 or .50cal MG, initially on a pintle mount in the middle of the vehicle. Both vehicles had quarter-inch face hardened steel armour. The main improvement of the new M2A1/M3A1 halftracks was the addition of a ring mount above the front 'shotgun' seat for the machine gun, eliminating the track and pintle mountings.

The M2/M3 was well-liked, or at least tolerated by its users in the infantry battalions of armoured divisions. It was a bit high-maintenance, very noisy, and the armour protection was inadequate. One veteran of the Tunisian fighting, when asked if the M3's armour could be penetrated by bullets, responded, 'No sir, it does not. As a matter of fact, bullets only generally come in one side and rattle around a bit.' The halftrack was not truly intended to be an infantry fighting vehicle, but simply a battle taxi; once near the fighting, the infantry learned to dismount rapidly. Experiments in increasing the armour or covering the top led to vehicle handling problems. In combat, GIs added sandbags to the floor (against mines) and machine guns to the sides. Racks for spare road wheels and miscellaneous gear were also attached to the outside hull, giving the mechanised infantry columns a distinctly 'gypsy' look.

Numerous variants of the M2/M3 were produced. One which attracted attention, if not affection, was the M3 75mm Gun Motor Carriage (GMC) used as a stop-gap anti-tank gun. The M3 75mm GMC saw extensive use in Tunisia, where it proved a very limited success; it was also used in smaller numbers in Sicily and Italy. It was thankfully replaced by the M10 tank destroyer as rapidly as possible. (The Tank Destroyer branch used the silhouette of the M3 75mm GMC as its insignia.) The anti-aircraft M15 mounted two .50cal machine guns and a 37mm gun; the M16 'quad-fifty' AA and M4 81mm mortar halftracks were also commonly seen variants. The M5 and M9 were produced by International Harvester for Lend-Lease and were almost identical to the M2 and M3 respectively.

Sicily, July 1943: a stretcher bearer from the 3rd Infantry Division holds a plasma bottle for a wounded GI. One of his 'dogtags' and his divisional patch are clearly visible. Since he wears the brassard, but no red cross on his helmet, he may be a rifleman temporarily assigned to this duty. Three men from the battalion's medical section were supposed to be attached to the headquarters of each rifle company.

MEDITERRANEAN THEATRE CAMPAIGN SUMMARY

Between 1942 and 1945 US troops and other Allied forces fought and won control in North Africa, Italy and France, before finally advancing into Germany and Austria on VE Day.

Morocco and Algeria

Three separate Allied landings under the command of Gen Dwight Eisenhower (Operation Torch, 8 November 1942) put 105,000 US and British troops ashore in Vichy French North Africa. In Algeria Gen Fredendall's Central Task Force landed near Oran and Gen Ryder's Eastern Task Force near Algiers. Both attempted a coup-de-main by taking ships and troops directly into harbours, but both attacks were checked by Vichy resistance led by the anti-British Admiral Darlan. After some sharp fighting Algiers and Oran surrendered on 8 and 10 November. In Morocco Gen Patton's Wesern Task Force landed at several points on the Atlantic coast; two of the three landings met stout resistance. Patton's commanders did not lose their nerve, however, and after some tight situations Casablanca surrendered on 11 November. Morocco cost the US Army 1,200 killed and wounded, but the landings proved to be a valuable 'live fire exercise' which highlighted the problems of amphibious warfare.

Tunisia

British 1st Army, US II Corps and pro-Allied French troops moved east into western Tunisia to take the German/Italian forces there – and those retreating westwards from Libya, pursued by British 8th Army – from the rear. II Corps (Gen Fredendall) consisted of 1st Armored and 1st, 9th and 34th Infantry Divisions. In mid-February 1943 Rommel's reinforced *Panzerarmee Afrika* broke the crust of the US defences around Sidi-bou-Zid and pushed through Kasserine Pass (20 February) to threaten Le Kef and the lone supply base at Tebessa. After early confusion and retreat, defensive fighting – both planned and spontaneous – slowed the attack and convinced the over-extended Germans to withdraw. The untried US Army had been bent at Kasserine, but not broken. The Allied command structure was reorganised; and after two and a half months of fighting the Axis forces surrendered on 11 May 1943. The aggressive American drive on Bizerta and Tunis in early May proved to any who doubted it the potential of the US Army. Coming so soon after the ruinous fall of Stalingrad, some among the quarter-million Axis prisoners referred to this new defeat as 'Tunisgrad'.

Sicily

In conjunction with Gen Montgomery's British 8th Army in the east, Gen Patton's US 7th Army landed on the south-west coast of Sicily on 10 July

North Africa, 1943: an Engineer officer from the 9th Infantry Division clears German explosives from a booby-trapped building. He wears an officer's wool shirt with epaulettes; note the Engineers' castle insignia on his left collar, and the divisional left shoulder patch.

1943. Bad weather and inexperience caused heavy losses and scattered landings for the airborne phase of the operation; the ground formations were the 1st, 3rd and 45th Divisions with three Ranger battalions. A spirited reaction from the Italian 'Livorno' and German 'Hermann Göring' divisions was decisively repelled with air and naval gunfire support. While the British slowly punched north towards Messina, 7th Army, reinforced with the 9th Division and part of the 2nd Armored, swung westwards, taking Palermo in a week. Driving eastwards across the top of Sicily, Patton closed in on Messina. Using small amphibious landings to outflank the growing opposition, US forces occupied

8 August 1944: soldiers from the 3rd Infantry Division embark on LSTs for the invasion of the South of France; they wear HBTs and M1928 packs. Apart from the divisional sign painted on both sides of their helmets they seem to have 'playing card' symbols on the back, probably identifying their battalions or companies.

the city on 17 August. Although the Germans suffered some 30,000 casualties, about 60,000 made a successful escape to the Italian mainland. The Sicily campaign cost the US Army just over 7,000 casualties.

Italy: Salerno

Italy secretly negotiated an armistice with the Allies, though this was not actually announced until 8 September 1943 – five days after the British XIII Corps crossed the Straits ofMessina to land on the 'toe' of Italy almost unopposed. On 9 September Gen Mark Clark's US 5th Army began landing at Salerno near Naples, with two US and two British divisions plus Commandos and Rangers. General Kesselring rapidly concentrated German forces and launched determined counterattacks, preventing consolidation of the four beachheads. Only a desperate defence and naval gunfire support stopped the most dangerous attack (12 September); further reinforcements, including a regimental drop by 82nd Airborne Division, helped stabilise the situation; and the slow Allied advance reached the Germans' Volturno defensive line just north of Naples on 8 October. Kesselring, with the terrain all in his favour, pulled back to the winter Gustav Line, running across the country roughly from Gaeta in the west to Ortona in the east. He continued to conduct a masterly delaying campaign in the face of a series of joint offensives by US 5th Army in the west and British 8th Army (Gen Leese) in the east, with increasing support from a French Expeditionary Corps. The key to the western sector of the Gustav Line was the Monte Cassino massif, which the Allies reached just before Christmas 1943.

Italy: Cassino

Cassino and the surrounding hills dominated a major road axis north to Rome through the Liri Valley. Defended mostly by the crack German paratroops of 1.Fallschirmjäger-Division and mountain troops of 5.Gebirgs-Division, it withstood five months of repeated Allied attacks. First unsuccessfully assaulted across the Rapido River in February 1944 by the US 36th and 34th Divisions, this bastion was bombarded by the Air Corps; repeatedly attacked by British, Indian and New Zealand troops; and finally – to the surprise of both Allies and Germans – made untenable by a strategic envelopment initiated by the French corps. The Germans made a fighting withdrawal in May 1944, and the mountain was finally taken by Polish troops. Canadian forces now joined the US and British armies for the next offensive up the Liri Valley.

Italy: Anzio

It was believed that landings at Anzio to the north, astride the German lines of communication, would force them to abandon the Gustav Line. The US VI Corps (Gen Lucas) with the 3rd and 45th Divisions, Rangers, and the British 1st Division landed unopposed on 22 January 1944, but were allowed by Gen Clark to dig in instead of immediately exploiting the surprise they had achieved. The Germans concentrated all their reserves onto the high ground surrounding the beachhead; throughout February they hammered the landing force, and by March the fighting had settled into a World War I style trench-bound siege.

With the fall of Cassino to the south the steadily reinforced beachhead broke out at the end of May – not east to cut off the retreating German 10th Army, however, but north, to seize Rome on 4 June. The bungled Anzio gamble cost the US almost 24,000 casualties. Gen Clark's failure to reinforce and exploit the landing, and his obsession with the purely symbolic capture of unde-fended Rome rather than destroying a significant part

Bill Mauldin was a private in the 45th Division with a talent for cartooning, who soon became the leading cartoonist for the GI-run *Stars and Stripes* magazine. His characters 'Willy and Joe' – Joe on the left here – quickly became favourites with the front-line soldiers. In this scene the captain is saying: 'I'm depending on you old men to be a steadying influence for the replacements.' (Reprinted by permission of Bill Mauldin & Watkins/Loomis Agency)

Bambiano, Italy, October 1944: the war is over for this barefoot Russian recruit to the Wehrmacht. His escort wears M1943 combat uniform, and has an illegible name or slogan chalked on the front of his helmet. He is armed with the M1 carbine, here with a grenade laucher muzzle attachment, and the M3 fighting knife.

Italy, 1944: a staff sergeant (right) from the 88th Infantry Division – note blue quatrefoil patch and rank insignia – talking to refugees. His buddy's medical haversack and their lack of weapons suggest that both are medics. Note the field jacket (or raincoat?) carried tucked under the GI's belt – a common sight.

of Kesselring's armies, ensured that the war in Italy would drag on into 1945.

South of France

The combined British/US 1st Airborne Task Force made a typically scattered parachute landing on the French Riviera on the night of 14/15 August 1944, and the next day the Allies began landing US 7th Army (Gen Patch) with the veteran 45th, 3rd and 36th Divisions and the 1st Special Service Force. The newly constituted French Army B (later 1st Army – Gen de Lattre) quickly reinforced the landings, which cost only some 200 US casualties. The weak, low priority German 19th Army was unable to prevent the US army from racing northwards, while De Lattre's French turned west to capture the ports. Patch cut off and all but destroyed the 19th Army at Montelimar on the Rhone, and Toulon and Marseilles fell to the Allies on 28 August. They were soon handling more supplies than all the Normandy ports combined, and proved a logistical life-saver for the continued Allied advance across France. Patch's 7th linked up with Patton's 3rd Army near Dijon on 11 September. The French 1st and US 7th Armies were organised into the 6th Army Group under the US Gen Devers (15 September), and served on the southern flank of the Allied armies, advancing through Alsace/Lorraine into Germany and Austria by VE-Day.

Northern Italy

After abandoning Rome in May 1944 the Germans slowly retreated to the prepared Gothic Line in northern Italy. With Gen Clark promoted to command 15th Army Group, comprising all Allied troops in Italy (24 November 1944), 5th Army was now capably led by Gen Truscott. By 1945 5th Army included the 10th Mountain, 34th, 85th, 88th, 91st and 92nd Divisions and 1st Armored Division. To the east, British 8th Army (Gen McCreery) combined British, Indian, Canadian and Polish divisions. In April 1945 both 5th and 8th Armies penetrated the Gothic Line, and all the cities of northern Italy fell into Allied hands by the end of the month. The German forces, now commanded by Gen von Vietinghoff, surrendered unconditionally on 2 May. The US 5th Army linked up with the 7th Army in the Brenner Pass on 4 May 1945.

1st Armored Division ('Old Ironsides'). Morocco, Tunisia, Anzio (Italy). Armored Force triangle with black '1'.

 1st Infantry Division ('Big Red One'). Morocco, Tunisia, Sicily, Normandy, France, Battle of the Bulge, Germany. Red '1' on bronze-green shield.

 3rd Infantry Division ('Marne'). Morocco, Sicily, Cassino, Anzio (Italy), South of France, Germany. Blue/white diagonally striped square.

 9th Infantry Division ('Varsity'). Morocco, Tunisia, Sicily, Normandy, France, Germany. Nine-petalled flower halved blue above red, white centre, all on khaki disk.

 10th Mountain Division ('Mountaineers'). Gothic Line, Po Valley (Italy). Crossed red swords edged white on blue rectangle edged white, below white-on-blue 'Mountain' tab.

 34th Infantry Division ('Red Bull' or 'Longhorns'). Morocco, Tunisia, Cassino, Gothic Line, Po Valley (Italy). Red bull's skull on dark blue Mexican flask shape.

 36th Infantry Division ('Texas'). Salerno, Cassino (Italy), South of France, Germany. Bronze-green 'T' on blue-grey Indian arrowhead.

 45th Infantry Division ('Thunderbirds'). Sicily, Salerno, Cassino, (Italy), South of France, Belfort Gap (France), Germany. Yellow Indian thunderbird on red triangle.

 82nd Airborne Division ('All American'). Tunisia, Sicily, Salerno, Anzio (Italy), Normandy, Battle of the Bulge, Netherlands, Germany. White opposed 'AA' on blue disk on red square, below white-on-blue 'Airborne' tab.

 85th Infantry Division ('Custer'). Rome, Po Valley (Italy). Red 'CD' on khaki disk.

 88th Infantry Division ('Blue Devils'). Liri Valley, Volterra (Italy), Northern Italy, Trieste. Solid blue quatrefoil.

 91st Infantry Division ('Powder River' or 'Pine Tree'). Gothic Line, Bologna, Gorizia (Italy). Green pine tree.

 92nd Infantry Division ('Buffalo'). Northern Italy. Black buffalo facing left on khaki disk edged black.

THE PLATES: MEDITERRANEAN

A: MOROCCO & ALGERIA, NOVEMBER/DECEMBER 1942

A1: Lieutenant-colonel, Ordnance, 2nd Armored Division

This 'short' colonel (addressed out of courtesy as 'Colonel') wears the standard khaki summer shirtsleeve uniform with officer's belt buckle. (Medal ribbons were also authorised to be worn with this shirt, though this officer chooses not to.) The brass flaming bomb insignia on his left collar point identifies him as serving in the Ordnance branch, responsible for weapons, ammunition, and the repair and maintenance of vehicles and hundreds of other GI items; in the 2nd Armored this element was provided by the former 17th Ordnance and 14th QM Bns combined into a single divisional Maintenance Battalion. Rank is shown by the silver leaf on his right collar and cap. This headgear is the khaki overseas cap, piped with mixed gold and black for officers, but he could also wear the khaki version of the leather-visored service dress hat. The patch of the Armored Force, with the divisional number, is worn on the left shoulder. After briefly fighting the Vichy French, in November 1942–January 1943 the 2nd Armored, garrisoned in Morocco, provided G and H Companies, 67th Armored Regt, to the British 78th Division fighting in Tunisia. The 'Hell on Wheels' division – whose main units were the 66th and 67th Armor, 41st Infantry, 82nd Recon Bn, 14th and 92nd Armored Field and 78th Field Artillery – would see its first major combat in Sicily, where it landed at Gela with the 1st Infantry Division on 10 July 1943.

A2: Infantry private, BAR gunner, 9th Infantry Division

Because of the bad blood between the British and the Vichy French caused by events earlier in the war, the Allied high command – who wanted the French garrison to recognise the Allied invaders as essentially friendly – ensured that US troops generally led the landings, and came ashore wearing white armbands and US flag shoulder patches or brassards. This infantry squad Browning Automatic Rifle gunner wears the standard first pattern herringbone twill (HBT) uniform, identified by its two-button waistband, buttoned cuffs and pocket details; later HBTs would have large breast pockets and thigh cargo pockets. Note the haversack for the M1A2 or M2A1 gasmask, marked with the symbol of the Chemical Warfare Service; and the BAR magazine belt with six large pockets. Veteran BAR gunners commonly dispensed with the M1918A2 weapon's extraneous features such as the bipod, to reduce its weight from 18 to 15lbs. This young soldier's eye glasses are the standard Army metal frame issue. He wears his helmet chinstrap buckled in the regulation manner; veterans soon violated this requirement for fear of literally losing their heads in the concussion of a shell burst.

A3: Sergeant, Military Police, II Corps

Each division had an MP company, and independent MP units were also assigned as corps and army assets. As enforcers of discipline and regulations, rear-area MPs inevitably had a reputation for officiousness and short tempers, and had few admirers among the GIs. This sergeant sports the standard white helmet markings and white-on-black armband used throughout the war. His khaki 'chino' service uniform was commonly worn in rear areas in the Mediterranean theatre; as part of a II Corps HQ guard detail he is neatly turned out, complete with necktie; and note the whistle and chain. Below the II Corps left sleeve patch his rank chevrons are machine-woven in dull silver on black. He is armed with the newly produced M1903A3 rifle, closely based on the World War I Springfield 03; and carries the early war M1905 long bayonet in the new OD plastic scabbard.

This MP wears the standard drab wool uniform and Parsons jacket with the addition of a tanker's helmet marked 'MP' and a brassard. His Harley has leather saddlebags and an M1 carbine in the scabbard. The censor has scribbled over some of the road signs.

The standard uniform for MPs almost invariably included steel helmets or liners marked with a broad white stripe with 'MP' at the front, and a white-on-black 'MP' left sleeve brassard. In army-level headquarter locations the MPs wore white leggings and webbing and all-white helmet liners, earning them the nickname 'Snowdrops'. MPs were commonly armed with .45 pistols and 03 rifles or M1 carbines.

B: TUNISIA, WINTER 1942/SPRING 1943

B1: Infantry sergeant, bazooka gunner, 1st Infantry Division

Winter in the Tunisian hills proved unexpectedly cold and wet, and GIs often wore the drab wool uniform underneath their HBTs for warmth. This 'buck sergeant' wears his HBT trousers over wool trousers; behind him lies his OD field jacket (the Parsons jacket, incorrectly called by modern collectors the 'M1941'), of cotton duck with an inadequate flannel lining; he may well be wearing woollen 'longjohns' too. On his drab wool shirt – note 'gas flap' at the neck – his rank is shown by dull silver chevrons on black backing; on his left shoulder is the 'Big Red One' divisional patch. His personal weapon is a holstered M1911A1 Colt .45 semi-automatic pistol, and he has added a civilian hunting knife to his belt kit. He carries the modified first pattern of the M1 bazooka, with the forward grip removed; his goggles are as much to protect him from the weapon's backblast as from the desert dust. Note the thick, pale edge of his early fabric-covered helmet liner. Both the 1st Infantry and 1st Armored Divisions were roughly handled by the Germans in the fighting near Kasserine Pass in February 1943.

B2: Infantry private, 1st Infantry Division

This assistant bazooka man wears the 'M1941' Parsons field jacket over his wool shirt and trousers. His issued helmet net can hold camouflaging vegetation or serve simply to soften the outline of the M1 helmet. Wearing standard rifleman's equipment – rifle cartridge belt with suspenders, aid pouch and canteen – this harebrained private has discovered that his cartridge pouches also serve as an ideal spot to carry the cigarette packs from his combat rations. He is armed with the M1 Garand and leather sling, the standard personal weapon of the GI by 1943, with – at this date – the long M1905 bayonet; an Mk II fragmentation grenade is fixed to his web

Stateside GIs at Camp Stoneman play baseball while wearing M1/M3 gasmasks, to accustom them to its discomfort. Gasmasks were developed and issued throughout most of the war; since the Allies were concerned that a desperate enemy might resort to chemical warfare at any time, masks were actually carried onto the beach in North Africa and Normandy. The Army started the war with the M1 rubberised face mask, hose and canister very similar to the World War I issue. An improved M2 Heavy Weight mask was also issued but was found too cumbersome at 5lbs (2.26kg). The M3 Light Weight mask (3lbs) came into use in 1943. The M4 mask, which went into production in 1944, was a revised Heavy Weight mask. All these models continued to use the hose and canister configuration.

The M5 Assault mask of 1944 was based on the German mask with the canister fitted directly to the cheek of the facepiece; this mask, stowed in a black rubberised carrier, was used in the D-Day landings – if properly closed the carrier also acted as a buoyancy aid for the wearer. An issue woollen gas hood was welcomed by GIs in winter; and the 1944 general issue gasmask carrier was also found to make a handy haversack.

belt suspenders. As the loader for the bazooka he carries one rocket (visible – others will be carried in a web bag). From World War II until today grenades, mortar bombs and bazooka rounds have all come issued in the same kind of stout black cardboard tubes.

B3: Sergeant of a tank unit, 1st Armored Division

To the envy of his infantry comrades, this NCO from the 1st or 13th Armored Regiment sports the wool-lined winter combat overalls and wool shirt as outer wear; like the vast majority of tankers, he has dispensed with his leggings. His

Armored Force shoulder patch bears the divisional number in the yellow upper section. (Independent tank battalions assigned as corps or army assets, which were identified by three-digit numbers, sometimes had their number custom-embroidered onto their un-numbered issue patches.) He is armed with a .45 holstered on his pistol belt, which also supports a two-clip ammunition pouch, and a World War I vintage aid pouch with a two-snap flap. The M1942 'armored forces' helmet', in hardened leather, was developed to protect crewmen from getting their brains beaten out against the many steel projections as they were bounced around inside a lurching tank; headphones are mounted into its earflaps, and a throat microphone rig was sometimes used. It is worn here over the padded 'winter combat helmet' in khaki fabric. The packaging of the Lucky Strike Green cigarette brand was changed to white during the war to save on green dye; it was said that 'Lucky Strike Green went to war, and didn't come back'. The 1st Armored Division – 'Old Ironsides' – served out the entire war in the Mediterranean theatre.

C: SICILY, SUMMER 1943
C1: Infantry private, machine gun crew, 3rd Infantry Division
This loaded-down private carries the 14lb (6.3kg) tripod for the Browning M1919A4; later in the war a BAR bipod was sometimes unofficially substituted for this. The metal ammo box with one 250-round belt weighed about 5lbs (2.25kg). A machine gun team needed at least three men to carry the weapon and particularly the ammunition; regulations called for five-man gun teams – any crew-served weapon used up

ammunition in large quantities. This GI is also burdened with his own M1 Garand; the standard cartridge belt carried 80 rounds of 30-06 ammunition, and the disposable six-pocket cloth bandoleer another 48 rounds. His bayonet is attached to the left side of his M1928 pack. Although HBTs were sometimes worn as combat clothing in summer, it was found that the woollen uniform could be tolerated during the day, and came in handy during the cold nights of spring and autumn. The 3rd ('Marne') Division – whose infantry regiments were the 7th, 15th and 20th – would have 531 days in combat, and would make five amphibious landings in World War II.

C2: Infantry corporal, machine gunner, 3rd Infantry Division
At 31lbs (14kg), the .30cal Browning M1919A4 air-cooled machine gun was 10lbs (4.5kg) lighter than its water-cooled M1917 predecessor, and came as a godsend to the infantry; each rifle company's weapons platoon had two guns. Its 250-round feed belt came in this unfortunate highly visible white cotton; this gunner's 'immediate use' belt has been cut in half to ease handling. Every fifth round came as red-tipped tracer, though veteran GIs would replace these with normal M2 ball to reduce the signature of the firer. For self-defence this corporal gunner is armed with a .45 pistol and the well-liked M3 combat knife. His standard wool shirt and trousers are in the drab colour described by 106th Division veteran Kurt Vonnegut as 'dogshit brown'; he displays silver-on-black rank chevrons and, on the left shoulder, the blue and white patch of the 3rd Division. This was not seen

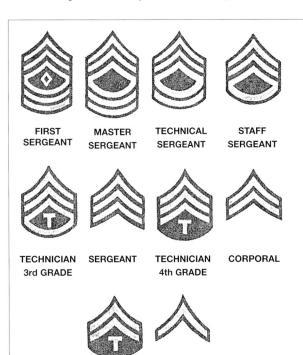

FIRST SERGEANT   MASTER SERGEANT   TECHNICAL SERGEANT   STAFF SERGEANT

TECHNICIAN 3rd GRADE   SERGEANT   TECHNICIAN 4th GRADE   CORPORAL

TECHNICIAN 5TH GRADE   PRIVATE 1st CLASS

NCOs' rank insignia
The 1st Sergeant (1Sgt) was the senior NCO in a company. After World War I the battalion rank of sergeant major – (SgtMaj) (Bn) – was eliminated, with master sergeants (MSgts) filling that role until the return of the sergeant major after the war. The lower arcs on senior NCOs' insignia are called 'rockers'. In 1941 the rank of first sergeant was marked by three chevrons above two rockers; in 1943 a third rocker was added.

NCO stripes were worn on both arms mid-way between the elbow and the shoulder. The common style available at the beginning of the war were in dull silver on black backing, and these were used on almost every form of combat and service dress. Also available were a version in OD green felt appliquéd on black, used on winter overcoats and wool shirts. In combat zones both types were used on wool shirts and combat jackets (M1941 and M1943). Bronze-coloured stripes on a khaki backing were sometimes used on 'chino' shirts but the silver-on-black pattern was much more common. In 1944 medium green stripes on black backing began to become available. These are most usually seen on the service coat and 'Ike jacket' late in the war.

The Army began experimenting with special technician ranks and pay in 1940. Technician ranks were created to reward soldiers who had technical skills such as medics, mechanics, cooks, radiomen, etc. They received slightly more money than their 'hard stripe' equivalents, but were considered junior to them in seniority.

painted on the sides of the helmet until after Sicily. His field jacket is carried tucked into the back of his belt, and he lugs a 250-round ammunition box in his free hand.

C3: Private first class, 3rd Ranger Battalion

The 1st, 3rd and 4th Ranger Battalions distinguished themselves as shock troops during and after the landings in North Africa, Sicily and Italy; on occasion they operated as an *ad hoc* brigade under command of LtCol William O.Darby, CO of the 1st Rangers, and at other times battalions were attached to the 1st, 3rd, 36th or 45th Infantry Divisions. In Sicily the 3rd Rangers were attached to the 3rd Division for the final push to secure Messina. On 30 January 1944 the 1st and 3rd Bns would be wiped out almost to the last man at Cisterna di Littoria near Anzio when surrounded by the elite Fallschirm-Panzer-Division 'Hermann Göring'.

The older bolt action M1903 was a favourite weapon of Col Darby, and individual Rangers continued to carry the 03 even after the M1 Garand was readily available (it was also the only weapon capable of propelling rifle grenades until mid-1944). This Ranger carries an M1903A3 and Mk II grenades; he wears standard drab wool shirt and trousers; and it was common in the Rangers to cut the M1938 leggings short by several inches for greater ease and general comfort. The Rangers also preferred the M1928 pack to any of the alternatives, as they felt it to be more comfortable on long marches. This private first class (Pfc) wears the winter-style chevrons in OD felt sewn to black backing, as commonly used throughout the war; above this on the left shoulder is the locally produced scroll-shaped Ranger battalion title, which several photographs show to have been worn in combat. Photos also show individuals with cleated boot-soles.

D: ITALY, 1943/44

D1: First lieutenant, Field Artillery, 36th Infantry Division

This artillery FO (Forward Observer) from the 36th Division – sometimes called the 'Texas Army' – wears the officer's version of the wool service shirt. Officers' shirts were usually differentiated by darker colours (anything between standard EM's drab to a dark chocolate brown), and the inclusion of epaulettes (shoulder straps). This fairly natty first lieutenant wears matching drab shirt and trousers; his branch is shown by brass crossed cannons on his left collar, his formation by the Texas division's shoulder patch. He is armed with an M1 carbine and a .45 pistol; his binoculars have a russet leather case. It was not intended that the carbine double clip pouch be worn on the weapon stock, but enterprising GIs soon made this modification. The 36th Division landed at Salerno and saw heavy fighting in Italy, eastern France and Germany until the end of the war. The divisional artillery units were the 131st, 132nd and 133rd Light and 155th Medium battalions. Special air-ground FO units – called 'Rover Joes' – were also used in Italy; these specialised in calling in air strikes on 15–20 minutes' notice.

D2: Technician 4th grade, 100th Battalion

The 34th 'Red Bull' Division was among the first to order its sign to be painted on the M1 helmet. The crack 100th Bn was made up of mostly Hawaiian Nisei (Japanese-American) National Guardsmen, whose unit motto was 'Remember

France, September 1944: combat-laden GIs from 3rd Division clamber up the embankment of the Doubs River. The lower man on the ladder has a BAR belt, two canteens, a two-pocket grenade pouch, and his Parsons jacket stuffed under his belt. (See Plate C.)

Pearl Harbor'. It joined the 34th Division in September 1943, spearheading two divisional attacks on Monte Cassino, and later served at Anzio; the unit subsequently became part of the Nisei 442nd Regimental Combat Team. (The other divisional infantry were the 133rd, 135th and 168th Regiments.) This Signal Corps 'tech sergeant' – who, although a technician, would be addressed as 'Sergeant' – is about to check with his wire-laying teams, using the SCR 536 'handie-talkie' radio. This had a single preset frequency and was turned on by extending the antenna; the theoretical effective range was about a mile. Installing lines and fixing breaks could be a disconcertingly hazardous duty under fire. This NCO is lucky to be armed with the M1 carbine – most Nisei carried the heavier M1 Garand throughout the war. His linesman's leather case containing wirecutters and knife is unofficially embellished with an officer's full colour Signal Corps insignia. (This kit is still in use by the Army, as is the WD-1 two pair field wire.)

D3: Staff sergeant, Field Artillery, 34th Infantry Division

This artillery NCO serving as an FO is using the leather-cased EE-8B field telephone to call for fire. The handy M1936 musette bag which he is using as a general purpose haversack could also be attached to the 'D' rings on the web suspenders and worn as a backpack. An L-head GI flashlight is visible clipped to his pistol belt. Though ranked as a 'staff' sergeant this NCO would most frequently serve as a platoon leader or even as first sergeant in a line combat outfit. Like all but the most senior NCOs he would be addressed as 'Sergeant', or even the familiar 'Sarge'. The workhorse 34th Division was recruited mainly from Minnesota and the Dakotas, and was the first Army division shipped to Europe; its artillery battalions were the 125th, 151st and 175th Light

and 185th Medium. The division would serve 517 days in combat in the Mediterranean theatre.

E: ANZIO, JANUARY 1944
E1: Medical orderly, VI Corps
This Medical Corps soldier lacks any insignia other than the helmet markings (one of several shapes used – square,

Medals for valour
The *Medal of Honor* (MoH) is the highest medal awarded for extraordinary gallantry above and beyond the call of duty against an enemy. The light blue neck ribbon and the medal were slightly modified in 1944. The 3rd Division were awarded the largest number, 22, including the award to Lt Audie Murphy, among the most highly decorated US servicemen of the war. Controversially, the Medal of Honor could also be awarded for service rather than valour. General Douglas MacArthur accepted such an award for his service in the Philippines; Gen Dwight Eisenhower refused to accept one for his service, as he believed that the Medal of Honor should only be granted for bravery.

The *Distinguished Service Cross* (DSC) was established in July 1918 to recognise acts of extraordinary heroism not deemed worthy of the MoH.

Displayed after World War I as a small star added to the 1918 Victory Medal ribbon for bravery, the *Silver Star* was established in 1932, retroactive to 1898, as a medal in its own right. It was awarded to those who had distinguished themselves by gallantry in action against the enemy. Multiple awards were distinguished by oakleaves ('appurtenances') on the ribbon.

The *Bronze Star* was created in February 1944 to recognise acts of bravery or merit (not involving flying). A bronze 'V' for valour was attached to the ribbon to distinguish awards for bravery from those for merit. The provision for awarding this medal for merit or service somewhat devalued it in the minds of combat GIs. (The Air Corps equivalent, the Air Medal, preceded the Bronze Star. It was established in May 1942, retroactive to 1939, to recognise acts of heroism or service involving aerial operations.) Oakleaves distinguished multiple awards of these medals.

The *Soldier's Medal* was created in 1926 for acts of heroism not involving combat but at the risk of ones own life.

The *Distinguished Unit Citation* was instituted in February 1942, for award to entire units for extraordinary heroism in action. The blue ribbon is framed in brass and is worn above the pocket on the right breast. Oakleaves distinguish multiple awards. This decoration was renamed the Presidential Unit Citation in 1957.

Combat Infantryman Badge
The Combat Infantryman Badge (CIB) and Expert Infantryman Badge (EIB) were created by the Chief of the Army Ground Forces, LtGen L.J.McNair, in October and November 1943. The CIB took the form of a silver musket on a light blue enamel plaque edged and wreathed in silver; it was awarded to infantrymen who

October 1944, South of France: 2nd Lt Barfoot, 157th Infantry Regiment, 45th Division, wearing his newly awarded Medal of Honor on its blue watered silk neck ribbon. On his EM's shirt he displays his rank bar on his right collar, the infantry rifles on the left, his Combat Infantryman Badge above the ribbon bars on his left breast, and the division's 'Thunderbird' patch on his left shoulder.

had served in combat for 30 days or who had been wounded in combat. The award was made retroactive to 7 December 1941. The EIB, similar but without the wreath, was awarded to infantrymen who had performed to a standard on the rifle range, in physical tests, and for proficiency in different combat-related tasks. Holders of the CIB and EIB received $10 and $5 a month respectively as an addition to their pay.

The CIB allowed combat infantrymen a distinctive badge that readily marked them as veterans. It could only be earned in combat by infantrymen or GIs officially serving directly in an infantry job, with medics, tankers and artillerymen excluded. (In 1945 an equivalent special Combat Medic badge was created.) The CIB was very popular among GIs, who sometimes took to proudly wearing it after VE-Day on their four-pocket M1943 field jackets.

'tombstone', etc.) and left arm brassard identifying his role. He wears the standard issue five-button pullover, drab wool trousers, and the newly issued and much appreciated M1943 combat service boots – 'buckle boots' – which did away with the need for leggings. Instead of the issue medical pouches he has a haversack-style gasmask bag which has been field-converted into an aid bag. Note the 'dog tags' hanging at his throat. This triage station is probably under intermittent artillery fire, as was everything else in the Anzio beachhead.

E2: Major of a tank unit, 1st Armored Division
Probably the second in command of a tank battalion, this major wears the sage green HBT one-piece overalls for combat, as was common in mechanised units (especially in hot weather – though in this case a sweater is visible at the neck). His rank and World War I tank Armored Force branch insignia are displayed on the collar of the HBTs. The unusual wearing of the divisional patch on the chest, as shown, was first encouraged by Gen Patton when he commanded the 2nd Armored Division in 1940, and is seen in a number of much later photographs. The use of the M3 shoulder holster was also common in tank units, as wearing waist belts could cause snagging inside the confines of a tank.

E3: Private first class, 1st Special Service Force
This regiment-sized unit successfully occupied a length of the front at Anzio normally held by a division. In southern France it was attached to the 1st Airborne Task Force; and was finally disbanded in November 1944. This Pfc wears the newly issued M1943 four-pocket OD green jacket, issued or 'scrounged' while at Anzio, where it was first field-tested; and the special mountain service trousers with thigh cargo pockets, common in the FSSF. The paratroop jump boots were also issue items to this parachute-qualified unit. He is armed with a wartime production M1 Thompson sub-machine gun with the new 30 round magazines; as the three-pocket 30-round magazine pouches were not yet available, GIs commonly used the five-pocket 20-round pouches, or a haversack. This soldier's V42 knife was particular to the FSSF and marks him as a 'Forceman' as clearly as his shoulder patch. **(Inset)** The crossed arrows branch insignia had previously been used by the Indian Scout units of the US Army. The 1st Special Service Force adopted both it, and the arrowhead unit patch, in commemoration of the Scouts; the Forcemen sometimes referred to themselves as 'braves' or the 'bow and arrow boys'. The 'Green Berets' of the US Army Special Forces resurrected the branch insignia and patch shape in the 1960s and use it to this day.

F: SOUTH & EAST FRANCE, 1944
F1: Captain, 1st Battalion, 551st Parachute Infantry Regiment, 1st Airborne Task Force
This Airborne officer wears the standard khaki M1942 paratroop uniform used in the first half of the war, in this case liberally striped with the OD green paint camouflage common to pathfinders and the 1st Airborne Task Force. His rank is shown only on his helmet; note also the painted camouflage, and the special web and leather airborne chin harness of the M1C model. The captain's weapons consist of a folding-stock M1A1 carbine, .45 pistol and Mk II grenade; an

While still in the USA an officer of the 1st Special Service Force receives his 'jump wings'. The FSSF crossed arrows branch insignia were custom-made for Col.Fredrick's outfit, copied from the insignia of the old Indian Scouts – and since copied by today's US Army Special Forces (see Plate E).

M3 fighting knife can just be seen tied to his left ankle. A musette is worn backpack style attached to the 'D'-rings of his suspenders, to one of which is attached his special aid packet containing both a bandage and a morphine syrette. The temporary 1st ATF – which lacked both vehicles and a logistics train – continued in front line service across south-eastern France well into the autumn of 1944 before being disbanded. It never had a patch, and the US flag worn on the shoulder served as its only insignia.

F2: Brigadier-general, US Army
As general officers were allowed a wide latitude in dress any number of variations might be seen from Eisenhower on down. Various US Army Air Corps jackets might be seen worn informally by general officers, and this one-star general has chosen to wear the glamorous A2 pilot's jacket in brown horsehide; note also the much sought-after 'Corcorans' – paratroop jump boots. His shirt is of the dark 'chocolate' shade, and his trousers are of dark shade OD wool almost matching it. Senior officers usually had their rank insignia

painted or mounted on the front of their helmets. He is armed with a .32cal ('general's model') M1903 Colt automatic worn in the M3 shoulder holster. Within a division this brigadier might serve as the second-in-command or as the divisional artillery commander.

F3: Infantry private first class, 45th Infantry Division

This rifleman, carrying K-ration cartons back to his squad, wears the new M1943 four-pocket field jacket but has not yet received the matching trousers; again, he does not display his rank chevron. Though officially only supposed to be worn under a helmet, the drab wool knit jeep cap or 'beanie' was a well-liked piece of GI headgear. In another departure from regulations this soldier has acquired a carbine to replace his M1 Garand – these were commonly seen in rifle companies by this stage of the war. Slung round his body is a general

A sniper checks his scope-sighted M1903A4 rifle. He is a reminder that front line soldiers are constant improvisers. He wears a loose-fitting home made burlap helmet cover to break up its silhouette, and his boots have been 'custom extended' by the addition of ankle sections.

RIGHT **France, October 1944: a staff sergeant and another GI take cover. The NCO wears the M1943 jacket with optional hood attached, and leather overgloves over knit wool gloves. Note the tape cross on the front of his helmet – he may be a medic.**

purpose ammunition bag, probably holding a steel 250-round machine gun belt box or rifle grenades. Wire cutters are carried on his belt, as is a captured Walther P-38 pistol; GIs sometimes carried 'hideaway' Lugers or P-38s in field-rigged shoulder holsters. The 45th 'Thunderbird' Division was a National Guard outfit based in the south-western states of the USA, which actually began the war with a Navajo swastika as its shoulder patch. It served in Sicily, Italy, southern and eastern France and Germany, and helped liberate the Dachau concentration camp. Its infantry regiments were the 157th, 179th and 180th.

G: ITALY, 1945
G1: Staff captain, 5th Army

Serving with 5th Army headquarters has given this staff officer access to the latest in winter wear. Though his rank bars show clearly on his helmet, many infantry officers smudged or painted over theirs to avoid drawing the enemy's attention. He sports a special issue cold weather coat-type hooded parka; this has two patch skirt pockets below two slash pockets and, unlike other parkas, it unbuttons all down the front (Gen Patton favoured this type of coat). Such outer garments were usually worn without insignia, but our spiffy captain has had the 5th Army patch added. A white pile liner with OD tape binding and knit cuffs was available for this parka. His trousers are the 18oz wool darker brown issue; and he has acquired a pair of the M1944 shoepacs – badly needed, and in short supply, for GIs in the winter mountains of northern Italy. Slung around his body is the officer's dispatch (map) case; and under the parka he probably carries a .45 pistol. Behind him lurks 'Kilroy', the ubiquitous character drawn on any suitable surface by GIs the world over. The original James J.Kilroy was a shipyard inspector who chalked 'Kilroy was here' when he approved a riveting job. Supposedly, military personnel boarding the new ships were intrigued when they found his mark everywhere – 'Kilroy always got there first'; and the craze for chalking it wherever troops arrived first spread all over the world.

G2: Master sergeant, 10th Mountain Division

Made up of outdoorsmen and skiers, the crack 10th Mountain Division was refused by Eisenhower for the ETO but was snapped up by Gen Clark's 5th Army. It especially

distinguished itself in the Po Valley fighting in March 1945. This NCO would be the senior enlisted man in his unit and would serve as a battalion sergeant major. He wears the limited issue Alpine-style second pattern anorak or 'ski parka'; this was reversible to white, and is otherwise identifiable by the fur trim around the hood only and the narrow buttoning flaps to the slash pockets. Like the mountain trousers which he also wears, it was peculiar to this division and the FSSF. Perhaps in the interests of ensuring that all his GIs get first chance at the available shoepacs, he still wears buckle boots (waterproofed?). He is armed with a carbine and M3 knife, and has decided to use a musette and a sleeping bag roll to carry his effects. The sergeant's helmet net is held down by the newly issued elasticated band.

G3: Infantry private, 10th Mountain Division

This private in either the 85th, 86th or 87th Infantry wears the special mountain troops' jacket, superficially similar to the four-pocket M1943 but with an integral belt and an expanding 'humpback' pack pocket on the back. The large chest pockets had zip fasteners under the flaps, and the skirt pockets were internally hung. He also wears the mountain trousers; leather-palmed wool gloves; and in place of the more common M1944 shoepacs, a pair of ski-mountain boots with 7in web ski gaiters secured by a crossed leather strap. He is armed with the M1 Garand, by this date issued with the 12in bayonet. This GI is heading for the woods to answer a call of nature, with a shovel – in this case a British GS type – and a dual-purpose copy of 'Yank' magazine.

(Background) Apart from the mountain rucksack, wood and plywood frame packboards were used throughout the Army and especially by the 10th Mountain Division. Jerrycans, rolls of wire, ration marmites, radios and ammunition were commonly man-carried using these frames.

H: PO VALLEY, 1945
H1: First lieutenant, 701st Tank Destroyer Battalion

This TD officer wears the wool-lined winter combat overalls and 1942 'tanker's jacket', with its knit waistband, cuffs and collar. His shirt collar shows his rank and the TD branch symbol; his jacket shoulder, the un-numbered patch common to all TD battalions. Tank destroyer crews – whose M10, M18 and M36 vehicles had open-top turrets – wore both the M1 and tanker's helmets. This lieutenant may be a platoon or company commander, depending upon his unit's recent rate of casualties. He is armed with a .45cal M3 'greasegun', the cheaper and simpler replacement for the Thompson SMG, which was standard issue to AFV crews. He is reading one of the range of handy phrasebooks/travel guides which the US Army produced for most of the countries where the GI might find himself.

H2: Infantry sergeant, 92nd Infantry Division

Even in Italy, where cold weather gear was a bit more available, the 32oz wool drab overcoat was still used until the end of the war for winter combat wear, partly due to the failure of the command and logistics chain to gather and forward the newer cold weather clothing to the front. This GI does at least have a pair of wool gloves and the new M1944 shoepacs, and wears his helmet over the knit wool 'beanie' cap. As a sergeant he could carry the M1 carbine if he

Italy, March 1945: troops of the 10th Mountain Division advance as the war nears its end. This GI wears the four-pocket mountain jacket with external belt and 'humpback' rear packpocket (see Plate G3). He may wear his web gear under it, or may be 'fighting out of his pockets'.

wished, but he prefers to keep the Garand rifle for the sake of its greater range and stopping power. As was very common, he uses an M2A2 gasmask bag as an all-purpose haversack; the shade contrasts with his greener late-war web gear. He is about to throw an M15 white phosphorus smoke grenade; apart from its 'Smoke/WP' marking, it is identifiable from other smoke canisters at night by feeling the domed bottom surface.

H3: Second lieutenant, 92nd Infantry Division

The African-American 92nd 'Buffalo' Division was officered mainly by southern whites; this black lieutenant is old for his rank. His helmet has no visible insignia, but by this date may have a large bar painted on the back to mark him out to following troops. His wool-lined cotton duck mackinaw coat – the wool-faced shawl collar identifying the first of three patterns, introduced in 1938 – was favoured by officers and vehicle drivers. His buckle boots are protected by four-clasp black canvas and rubber overshoes. As was common among line officers, his insignia of rank and branch are worn on his shirt collar only and are thus hidden when in the field. He carries his kit in a slung musette bag; among his belt equipment are a compass pouch attached below a carbine clip pouch, and a folding-head entrenching shovel. He has armed himself with an M1 carbine with the M8 grenade launcher muzzle attachment; this use put a strain on the stock, which here has been prudently bound with copper wire to prevent cracking – standard British practice, which he has perhaps copied. When rigged for launching the MkIIA1 fragmentation grenade had a range of about 250 yards.

This portrait of a war-weary sergeant is typical of a US tanker in the ETO in the winter of 1944/45. Note the connector jack on his right shoulder, hanging from his helmet; this connector pulled out easily if a crew had to abandon a burning tank in a hurry. Shortly after this photo was taken its subject, Sgt John H.Parks from Mill Creek, Indiana, was killed in action in Germany.

THE GIS WHO HIT 'Omaha' and 'Utah' beaches on 6 June 1944 were members of the finest-equipped mechanised army ever assembled. As Allied, and particularly American strength continued to build up in Normandy, the threadbare but still potent Wehrmacht soon came to realise they had an elephant by the tail. After the August break-out from Normandy and the landings in the south of France the ever more powerful US armies aggressively pursued the Germans across France in a classic demonstration of exploitation warfare. Even so, in some quarters there was still some jealous questioning as to the professionalism and endurance of the lavishly supplied and self-confident GI. Some British and German leaders, harking back to the US Army's blooding at Kasserine Pass in February 1943, wondered if the Americans would prove to have a glass jaw when the going got tough. (This was not, it must be said, a doubt harboured by any who had seen the fighting in Normandy from close up, from either side of the front.) The Battle of the Bulge in December 1944 would be the test.

Heavily attacked by superior German armour, outnumbered and without air support, the US Army was on its own in the Ardennes. A large portion of the green 106th Division held its position for a short time and then gave way in the biggest US surrender since Kasserine. The surprised Americans bent – but did not break. Bastogne was stubbornly held, and Germany's finest remaining Panzer troops were constantly bedevilled by skilled US delaying actions. By 1 January 1945 the Wehrmacht had suffered crippling losses without even approaching their objective, and the line was soon restored. The Battle of the Bulge had proven the battle worthiness of the GI, and was, in Prime Minister Churchill's words, 'truly an American victory'.

Supply crisis in the ETO

Despite America's apparently limitless manufacturing capacity and generous scales of issue for almost every necessity, one factor had a baleful effect on US operations – and on the daily conditions faced by many US soldiers – throughout NW Europe in the second half of 1944. The problem was not producing what was needed, or shipping it to Europe; it was getting it out of the ships and up to the front-line units when, where and in the quantities required. The overall supply situation in the ETO was poor, due in about equal measure to shortages of transportation and bad decisions on logistics taken by the staff at SHAEF (Supreme Headquarters Allied Expeditionary Forces).

Eisenhower's staff had planned for a steadily progressing advance with the Allies reaching the German border in early 1945. This would give time to clear the ports in western France and to move supplies

Ardennes, December 1944: coming in from manning a night roadblock, these three GIs (including two carrying bazookas) are lucky to have cold/wet weather footwear – in the foreground, four-clip M1942 overshoes. The man on the left wears the big fitted woollen anti-gas hood for warmth. From the diamond shape of the shoulder patch on the centre man's overcoat these soldiers could be from the 5th or 26th Divisions.

forward in a timely fashion. While the battle for Normandy ran behind schedule, the leap across France in August/September 1944 quickly outran all logistical planning. With the now distant ports still slow to clear, supplies continued to come in over Omaha beach. The 'Red Ball Express' priority trucking route (so named for the red mark used in the 1930s on priority railroad cars) gave some relief, as did the use of aircraft for cargo runs to the front. Railroads would have been the most efficient means of transport, but France's network, ripped up by Allied bombing in the weeks before D-Day, took a long time to rebuild. The opening of southern French ports after the 'Anvil' landings in August made some difference; but the failure of the British/Canadian Twenty-First Army Group to seize the estuaries at Antwerp, the greatest port in the Low Countries, left the Allies logistically adrift. The grand pursuit across France by the 1st and 3rd US Armies, and by Twenty-First Army Group in the Netherlands, ground to a standstill in September; and each of the Allied army commanders sought to pressure SHAEF into granting him priority of supply as they argued over the conflicting strategies of 'narrow thrust' and 'broad advance'. Such absolute basics as ammunition and gasoline became critical items. Eisenhower opted to bring ashore more combat units, but the transport to move them to the front was already consumed in running supplies to meet existing demands. Some 60 to 100 cargo ships collected off Cherbourg, waiting for dock space; and in September it began to get rainy and cold.

Stocks of gas, ammunition, blankets, tyres and winter uniforms all became critically short. The new buckled combat boot was now being issued, and it was felt that if treated with dubbin it would serve well enough as a winter boot for France. The war, however, was in Belgium, on the German border and in the Vosges mountains. The new boots were found to have little capacity to resist water or give warmth. With the Battle of the Bulge raging in December, winter overshoes and shoepacs became a priority; during that month the US Army in the ETO lost 56,000 men to non-battle causes such as frostbite and trench foot – by January 1945 these losses were almost equal to battle casualties. Winter boots finally arrived in significant numbers by late January. Overcoats and the new M1943 four-pocket combat jackets were also in short supply, since they had not been ordered or brought forward from the rear area Communications Zone (COM Z). The winter of 1944/45 also caught the US Army with few white camouflage suits (reversible anoraks) available at the front. White cotton bedsheets were pressed into service, cut and sewn by local civilians, QM and the GIs. Besides whitewashing vehicles and helmets, some men actually oversprayed their uniforms and equipment. Issue hooded snow camouflage suits finally began to appear in January. With the rapidly approaching spring the demand for such special items receded; and the Belgian ports also began to open.

SERVICE DRESS

Enlisted men

The US Army started the war wearing the M1939 four-pocket drab brown 18oz wool serge coat and trousers for service dress (Class A). Until the issue of the M1941 Parsons field jacket this was also intended to be one of the Army's field uniforms. The coat had two patch breast pockets and two inside skirt pockets, both with flaps. The back had bi-swing shoulder gussets, belt hooks and an integral cloth belt across the small of the back. A russet leather belt with plain brass bar buckle was to be worn with the coat until its deletion in 1941. The open lapelled front of the tunic closed with four 1-inch diameter brass buttons bearing the eagle seal of the US; half-inch eagle buttons were used for the pockets and epaulettes. In 1942 the simpler M1942 coat, without a bi-swing back, became the standard issue.

Rank insignia were sewn on both sleeves above the elbow in OD green on black felt; silver-on-black stripes were also used. The four-pocket coat was made limited standard in September 1944 in favour of the M1944 wool field or 'Ike' jacket.

Creased wool serge trousers (M1939) were worn with the service coat, usually of the same or a slightly lighter shade of drab brown. In the ETO the drab, long-sleeved wool shirt was worn initially with a black but more commonly with a khaki necktie. The shirt had two breast pockets with clipped flaps and a buttoned front and cuffs. With the issue of the slightly darker 'Ike' jacket in 1944/45, both the older pants and newer matching equivalents were to be seen. Russet leather ankle boots or shoes were worn with the four-pocket service dress; with the new 'Ike' jacket, shined buckle boots were commonly worn; trousers were tucked into the boots paratrooper-style, or worn loose with low quarter shoes. Most shirts and pants were made with an extra length of material behind the buttonholes; this 'gas flap' would supposedly protect the skin against blistering agents.

A brown drab visored or 'saucer' hat with a russet leather visor was the initial issue service dress hat. A flat sidecap – the 'overseas' or 'garrison cap' – in brown drab and summer/tropical khaki versions was soon authorised and became the standard issue. Initially, the edges of the turn-up flap or 'curtain' round the base of the cap were piped in branch-specific colours, and a regimental crest or branch-of-service collar disc was sometimes worn on its left front. Piping soon became optional, and unpiped caps were commonly seen. The popular overseas cap was cheap, light and easy to pack; it acquired a nickname based on the female anatomy.

Officers

The M1940 officer's hip length tunic ('coat') was generally similar to the enlisted version. It used a wool/barathea material of approximately 15-26oz weight, with a softer feel than the enlisted man's wool serge. The colour can best be described as a dark greenish/chocolate brown (officially, OD 51 dark shade). The breast pockets were pleated; the M1940 had bi-swing or pleated back seams and four brass buttons down the front. It was commonly worn with a russet Sam Browne belt with the crosstrap and twin-tongued thick bar brass buckle.

October 1944: this retiring 5th Division master sergeant wears the four-pocket M1942 dress coat (tunic). The left sleeve shows below the rank insignia the five bars marking two-and-a-half years' overseas service in World War II; the three chevrons of one-and-a-half years' overseas during World War I; and ten re-enlistments. Below this is the officer's drab braid cuff trim, signifying his previous commissioned service in World War I. The light streak on the breast pocket is a scratch on the negative.

The M1942 coat eliminated the bi-swing back and replaced the bottom button with a smooth plastic one, which fitted under an integral cloth waist belt with a slip-through brass buckle, replacing the Sam Browne. Officers' tunics also spor-ted a half-inch wide drab cloth braid around each cuff. Warrant officers wore the same tunic with greenish cuff braid. Beige/khaki trousers or breeches – called 'pinks' – were to be worn with this tunic.

Russet brown shoes, khaki shirt and black (early) or khaki necktie completed the uniform. This outfit was sometimes called 'pinks and greens'; and it was said by some British – in rueful jest, given their own clothes rationing – that Yank officers were obviously not as rich as everyone said if they couldn't afford to buy uniforms with matching trousers.

Greenham Common airfield, UK, 5 June 1944: one of the famous sequence of photos showing the Supreme Commander Allied Expeditionary Forces, Gen Dwight D.Eisenhower, with men of the 101st Airborne Division. Speaking here to a lieutenant, 'Ike' wears the jacket he made famous; the paratroopers wear their M1942 uniforms, with tactical helmet markings – here the white heart of the 502nd PIR. The right-hand man has a general purpose ammo bag slung on his chest.

ETO jacket

When the first GIs arrived in England in 1942 they saw the British battledress uniform (BD). A limited number of BDs were issued to the Americans; and their warmth, and the neat appearance which could be achieved with the waist-length two-pocket blouse, was well liked. (US senior officers were presumably judging not by the coarse serge 'Other Ranks' issue blouse, but by the privately tailored versions worn by their British counterparts.) By regulation US general officers are given a wide latitude in personal dress; Gen Eisenhower especially liked the short blouse, and had a sort of American version tailored for his own use, with a tighter fit and smoother cloth than the serge original.

The ETO staff then began to push for an American version, and in 1943 the ETO Quartermaster brought out the first model; this was essentially a version of the 'M1941' Parsons field jacket but made of the same rough, heavy-textured wool serge as the BD, warm and easy to care for. It featured exposed plastic buttons, 'handwarmer' pockets with flaps, a buckle-across waist tab and bi-swing back pleats. The second model to be produced looked more like a standard British BD blouse, with exposed plastic buttons, flapped patch breast pockets, epaulettes and a bi-swing back pleat. The ETO jacket was not an uncommon sight, particularly among Air Corps units in Britain. The QM in the States could not get the rough BD wool serge, but was making its own plans for a short blouse-style jacket.

M1944 'Ike' jacket

Based on recommendations from the ETO, the QM in the USA designed a short version of the four-pocket service coat. This new jacket was made from a slightly darker drab material; matching trousers with flapped rear pockets were also manufactured. The jacket had epaulettes, two pleated breast pockets with pointed flaps, buttoned cuffs, all buttons concealed, and a belted waist with take-up buckles on each hip. Unlike the British issue BD blouse, but like the ETO jacket, it also featured open lapels. The QM intended for this jacket to serve as both a field and service jacket replacing the four-pocket tunic; GIs were suppose to have it loose fitting for field wear, and to use it as a liner under the M1943 four-pocket combat jacket. However, the GIs had other ideas: they had it tailored tight and wore it almost exclusively as a service jacket.

This 'wool field jacket' first began limited issue in mid-1944 and was an immediate success, being universally nicknamed after the general who had shown the way. Because of limited availability, many GIs based in England had their four-pocket service tunics cut and retailored into a brass-buttoned version of the short 'Ike' jacket. After VE-Day GIs were issued the M1944 jacket almost exclusively. Rank was worn on both sleeves; insignia were in OD green on black felt, silver on black, or, more commonly, the newer green-on-black version.

An officer's version of the 'Ike' jacket was produced in dark green/chocolate (OD shade 51) and was worn with appropriate insignia; the officer's cuff trim was usually in a dark shade. This jacket – of which custom-tailored variations were also seen – was worn with either matching trousers or 'pinks'.

Branch colours and insignia

Each branch within the US Army had its own distinctive colour. This colour was only normally seen on flags, in some of the embellishments on officers' dress blue uniforms, in the cord piping on the curtain of enlisted men's overseas caps, and in the cords of the old campaign hat.

Each branch also had its own collar insignia. For officers these were of cut-out design, normally in brass but in some cases with additional coloured enamelling; chaplains' insignia were silver. They were worn on both lower lapels of the officer's service coat, below cut-out 'U.S.' national cyphers on the upper lapels. When in shirtsleeve order the branch badge was pinned to the wearer's left collar and the rank insignia to his right. Enlisted men wore the national cypher and the branch insignia on brass discs on the right and left upper lapels respectively.

The colours and insignia of the major branches normally encountered in combat zones are described in the table on page 104.

Distinctive insignia

Many units were authorised to wear heraldic-style crests in coloured enamels, which were sometimes displayed in the ETO on the officers' and enlisted

Normandy, summer 1944: an officers' orders group at a battalion HQ of the 29th Division (the censor's pen has scribbled over the right-hand man's patch). All wear the so-called 'tanker's jacket'; the man sitting in the middle has a fighting knife sticking out of his custom-made buckled leather legging. The kneeling man has British-made hobnailed boots, and an officer's bar painted on his helmet back; in the ETO all officers and NCOs were supposed to have a 2in-wide white bar painted here, vertical for officers and horizontal for NCOs. While not universally applied, these were commonly seen throughout 1944/45.

men's service dress when out of the line. They were displayed by officers centred on the service coat epaulettes, top inwards, and by enlisted men on the lower coat lapels; EMs could also pin one to the left front of the overseas cap.

Shoulder patches

During the American Civil War the Union Army began to use cloth identification patches, distinctively shaped for each corps and coloured for each division, and normally worn on the headgear. The British Army used many complex systems of distinctive sleeve patches at battalion, brigade and divisional level during World World I; these 'battle badges' were normally geometric shapes in solid colours, identifying units within a formation by their colour, shape and number. General Pershing also authorised the use of shoulder patches within the American Expeditionary Force in France, but the war ended as they came into issue. These differed from most of the British systems in being actual insignia

rather than systems to identify units. By World War II the use of such patches – officially, 'shoulder sleeve insignia' – within the US Army was common.

A division used a standard patch throughout its organisation, usually based on the previously designed World War I patch. In general these were embroidered multi-coloured patches, worn at the top of the left sleeve. The symbols used ran the gamut from heraldic designs, through visual references to the home state, to punning plays on words. Independent units, corps and armies also used patches, as did the Army Air Corps. Corps patches were normally blue on white, and commonly used Roman numerals. Those GIs not assigned to specific divisions usually wore corps or army patches.

Airborne units displayed an additional 'Airborne' title above their patch to show their status; they also wore a parachute, glider, or later a combined patch on their overseas caps. All armoured divisions and independent tank battalions used the triangular

SELECTION OF ARMY BRANCH COLOURS & INSIGNIA

Branch	Colour/s	Insignia
Army Air Force	Ultramarine piped w. golden yellow	Wings & propeller
Armored	Green piped w. white	WWI tank
Cavalry	Yellow	Crossed sabres
Chaplains (all-officer branch)	Black	Cross (Christian); Two tablets & Star of David (Jewish)
Chemical Warfare Service	Cobalt blue piped w. golden yellow	Benzol ring & crossed retorts
Coast Artillery	Scarlet	Crossed cannon, shell in red oval
Engineer Corps	Scarlet piped w. blue	Castle
Field Artillery	Scarlet	Crossed cannon
Infantry	Light blue	Crossed rifles
Medical Dept	Maroon piped w. white	Caduceus
Military Police	Yellow piped w. green	Crossed pistols
Ordnance Dept	Crimson piped w. yellow	Flaming shell
Quartermaster Corps	Buff	Eagle surmounting wheel, crossed sword & key
Signal Corps	Orange & white	Crossed signal flags & flaming torch
Tank Destroyer units	Golden orange	M3 SP gun (halftrack)
Transportation Corps	Brick red piped w. golden yellow	Winged car wheel, on shield, on ship's wheel
Women's Army Corps	Old gold piped w. moss green	Head of Athena

D-Day, Utah beach: two 4th Division medics work on a wounded comrade. Note the 'Ivy' patch on the left shoulder of the casualty's HBTs – not a usual practice in Normandy. The wounded medic still wears his assault gasmask and yoke-style web harness. Medics generally went in on D-Day wearing a minimum of red cross markings.

Armored Force patch divided red/yellow/blue (for the antecedent artillery, cavalry and infantry branches) differenced by divisional and unit numerals. (It was only after VE-Day that they began to add strips to the bottom of their triangular patches bearing their nicknames, the 2nd Armored Division's 'Hell on Wheels' being among the first seen.)

Patches were machine-embroidered onto khaki cotton cloth; original World War II patches sometimes show the khaki around the edges, and have a soft off-white rear surface. Some patches were fabricated overseas by local tailors, and bullion-embroidered versions were sometimes available. GIs who served in combat with more than one organisation were authorised to wear the patch of their original combat unit on the right shoulder of the service dress, at the same time as the current patch on the left.

Fourragères

In World War I both the 1st and 2nd Infantry Divisions were awarded the right to wear a *fourragère* or French-style left shoulder cord, in the green flecked with red of the Croix de Guerre ribbon, as a collective decoration to mark their service to France. In World War II members of those divisions were also authorised to wear it as a remembrance of their forbears' service, but this was rarely seen; actual World War I veterans still in service sometimes wore the fourragère, however.

During World War II the French began once again to award the fourragère to US units; the great majority of these awards were made near the end of the war. When seen worn by GIs the cords tended to be of the old World War I issue; the fourragère for the World War II Croix de Guerre had a slightly different coloration, of red flecked with green, and was in particularly short supply. Post-war GIs wore both kinds. Availability of these items from ruined and only recently liberated France was naturally disorganised. There were two design variants; one was a simple plaited cord, intended to be worn from the left epaulette button down the back of the shoulder, passing forward under the armpit and fixing by a loop to a front button, with a hanging brass ferrule. The other, more elaborate version had a long extra length of smooth cord which was supposed to be arranged under the epaulette so as to hang on the outside of the arm in two loops. Unknowing GIs did wear them on the correct shoulder, but in any number of ways. These cords were also awarded by the Belgian and Dutch governments. The red/green Belgian Croix de Guerre fourragère was worn on the right shoulder; the orange cord of the Dutch Wilhelm's Order was worn on the left, passing into the breast pocket. (Examples are illustrated on Plate H.)

Most units seem to have been semi-officially notified of their authorisation to wear these distinctions soon after VE-Day. It commonly took until the 1950s for the official orders authorising these awards to be confirmed.

Women's Army Corps

Women's Army uniforms were almost universally condemned for their poor fit and appearance. By VE-Day, however, they had some of the most practical and best-looking uniforms of any of the women's services. The 1942 drab service dress for enlisted WAACs/WACs consisted of a hip-length tunic with four brass buttons, in the same drab brownish colour (OD shade 54) as used by male personnel. It had scallop-flapped internal breast pockets and plain slashed lower pockets. A skirt reaching to just below the knee, and the stiff-billed 'Hobby' hat, were both in matching drab brown. A russet brown shoulder-purse was issued to be carried with this uniform. WAAC/WAC officers wore the same general style as the enlisted women.

Their coat and hat were made of wool barathea in the Army officers' dark green/chocolate colour (OD shade 51), and worn with a skirt made in the colour of officers' 'pinks'. The first coat issued had transverse shoulderstraps and an integral belt; the later model had normal epaulettes and no belt. In service dress, WACs wore sensible russet brown laced low-heel shoes, and sometimes brown gloves.

With the 1943 enrolment of the Auxiliaries of the WAAC into the regular Army the new Women's Army Corps dropped their 'walking buzzard' insignia in favour of the standard US eagle. They retained the use of the Athena head branch insignia, though many WACs serving with a specific branch – e.g. the Air Corps – wore that collar insignia instead.

In late 1944 WACs in Europe followed the current fashion, receiving a specially designed 'Ike' jacket with a matching skirt, trousers, and an overseas cap of more curved shape than the men's (see Plate D1). This jacket was modelled on the GI issue field/service jacket, both with and without breast pockets. It was made in both enlisted drab and officer's dark green/chocolate colours, and proved very popular. Like the men's version, the WACs' short jacket soon became the standard issue for the 'GI Jane'.

An off-duty dress was authorised in 1944 consisting of a fairly plain-looking, long-sleeved, knee-length dress of wool crêpe. This came in both beige (summer) and dark khaki (winter) colours; it had concealed buttons, a belt, patch breast pockets and epaulettes. Basic branch insignia were worn on the collar. A standard issue drab or matching beige overseas cap was worn with this dress.

A wounded lieutenant of the 506th PIR, 101st Airborne Division is helped ashore from an LST at Southampton, England, on 9 June 1944. At left, a trench-coated lieutenant carries his web belt, complete with the canvas scabbard for a folding-stock M1A1 carbine. The black medic wears the issue raincoat.

Again, note the white 'playing card suit' tactical marking on the sides of the injured officer's helmet – a common practice in the Airborne, to distinguish regiments and sub-units. All officers were to have their rank painted or mounted on the helmet front, like these two lieutenants; after D-Day this was commonly ignored by front-line leaders. Helmet nets of various types were issued throughout the ETO, with finer-mesh examples used from late 1944; elasticated helmet bands were to be seen in 1945.

Army Nurse Corps

The ANC was an auxiliary organisation originating in the Spanish-American War. These nurses were essentially contracted medical professionals who were, like the WAAC, finally given full Army status in 1943/44. They started the war wearing a dark blue tunic and skirt service uniform. Their working outfit was the classic white dress with nurse's cap and blue wool cape with red lining. They also used a seersucker white and brown striped work dress with insignia. In 1944 the ANC converted to the standard WAC uniforms available at that date. Standard officer insignia were worn, with a branch emblem of a brass caduceus with a superimposed black 'N'; most nurses were second lieutenants, but were paid less than their male Army counterparts. Nurses had a plain beige off-duty dress – this was in fact copied by the WAC (see above). The front of the nurse's service dress hat was similar to the WAC 'Hobby' hat, but the back was rounded to the crown.

England, 1944: HM Queen Elizabeth with a WAC officer and senior NCO. The captain wears her bars on the left front of the gold-piped WAC officer's overseas cap and on her tunic epaulettes, the Athena branch insignia, and the ribbons of the ETO and WAC medals. The first sergeant wears the generic ETO shoulder patch, and a year's worth of overseas service bars. (See also Plate D1.) Note the strong contrast between the dark officer's and lighter enlisted ranks' tunics.

ORGANISATION

Corps, Armies and Army Groups

A corps consisted of a minimum of two divisions. In the order of battle of the US Army in the ETO in 1945 we find about 18 corps – the uncertainty over the exact number lying in the presence of a number of divisions under direct command of an army. Most of these corps had three divisions, some four, one five and one – XVI Corps of 15th Army – had six. A representative example is Gen Walker's XX Corps of 3rd Army, which comprised four divisions – the 4th and 6th Armored, and 76th and 80th Infantry. In addition a corps normally had many independent units of tanks, artillery, engineers and other specialists under direct command.

An army was formed from two or more corps. Ten armies were formed for service in World War II. The 2nd and 4th Armies were stationed in the US and consisted of divisions under formation. By 1945 the last of the divisional units based in the US had left these two armies and were headed for the front. The 1st, 3rd and 9th Armies served in France, Belgium and Germany. The 7th Army served in Sicily, the South of France and Germany. The 5th Army was stationed in Italy. The 6th and 8th Armies served in the Pacific, with the 10th formed on Okinawa. As an example, in 1945 Gen Hodges' 1st Army consisted of III, V, VII and XVIII (Airborne Corps) and totalled 17 divisions.

Army groups were formed with a minimum of two armies. In 1945 the Twelfth Army Group (Gen Omar Bradley) consisted of the 1st and 3rd Armies (Gens Hodges and Patton). The US 9th Army (Gen Simpson) was traded back and forth between the Twelfth and the British/Canadian Twenty-First Army Group (Gen Montgomery). The Sixth Army Group (Gen Jacob Devers) consisted of the 7th Army (Gen Patch) and 1st French Army (Gen de Lattre). The Fifteenth Army Group

(Gen Mark Clark) was made up of the 5th Army (Gen Truscott) plus all the other Allied forces in Italy. In the Pacific, Army units served under Theater Commanders (Gen Douglas MacArthur and Adm Chester Nimitz). Supreme Headquarters Allied Expeditionary Forces (SHAEF) commanded all ground forces in Europe (Gen Dwight Eisenhower).

Rotation of divisions

In World War I entire divisions were withdrawn from combat for periodic rest and rebuilding. In the Pacific in World War II the short, violent battles for island groups and the time lag between invasions helped accomplish this rest cycle for Marine and some Army units. In the Mediterranean, Sicily fell in 30 days and the preparations for the Salerno and Anzio landings gave 5th Army units a reasonable chance to rest. In the ETO, and later in Italy, this cycling of units for rest was the exception.

Once a division was committed into combat, it was expected to stay at the front. During the war the 1st Infantry Division spent 442 days in combat, of which 317 days were served in the ETO. In France and Germany alone the 'Big Red One' lost 206 per cent of its strength to casualties; 85-90 per cent of this loss was from the three infantry regiments. During the 2nd Infantry Division's 314 days of ETO service it lost 184 per cent of its strength. Among those infantry divisions which entered combat in Normandy and fought through the eleven months to VE-Day, the average loss was about 200 per cent of establishment.

This rate of casualties had a terribly wearing effect on units, and gave the ever-dwindling handful of old hands an even more fatalistic view of their fate than usual. As the war dragged on it seemed that only a 'million dollar wound' was going to get a GI out of the war with all his limbs. The exception was the Airborne force (82nd and 101st Divisions). They did suffer severe losses, and were kept in the line for longer than they should have been after D-Day, but they were pulled out of the line to keep them available for future airborne operations.

Metz, late November 1944: riflemen and a BAR gunner from the 5th Division check houses for enemy 'stay-behinds'. Notice that only one wears a pack (to which he has strapped a K-ration box) and the others have their blankets, raincoats or ponchos stuffed through the back of their belts. The Germans turned Metz into a fortress which held up the Allied advance for many weeks; it finally fell to XX Corps of Gen Patton's 3rd Army on 22 November after a fortnight's hard fighting. At that time MajGen Walton Walker's XX Corps consisted of MajGen Stafford Irwin's 5th Infantry Division, the 90th Infantry Division, the 7th Armored Division, and the 2nd Cavalry Reconnaissance Group; but divisions were often switched between corps at short notice, and by the following spring XX Corps' composition was entirely different.

Replacements

The giant olive drab machine needed a constant flow of additional troops to keep up its strength. The AEF in World War I solved this problem by disbanding about every fourth division arriving in France and redistributing its men. In World War II the Army refused to allow this, and depended on individuals sent from the US to fill the gaps. Emphasising its machine-like viewpoint, the Army called these men 'replacements'. In 1944 the number of men individually

trained for posting as replacement parts rapidly fell short of the needs of the ravenous armies in France. The units based in the USA were soon mercilessly plundered. This weakened these training units, and sent bewildered replacements forward to units with which they had no connection. The semi-trained GIs lurched through the system until they arrived at forward replacement depots, called 'Repple-Depples'. Here combat-experienced GIs, sent forward again after recovering from wounds, mingled with the green replacements for days or even weeks as they awaited new assignments.

January 1945: a 'lost patrol' of the 94th Division pose for a photo, happy to be back in the fold and getting canned rations. Both Parsons and M1943 field jackets can be seen, and note the 94th's patch worn by the medical tech-corporal at right foreground. At left centre, the BAR man's weapon still has its bipod (often discarded), and he carries the cleaning kit on his belt. Peering over his shoulder is a dark-bearded veteran; the smooth-faced boy at extreme left is probably a more recent replacement.

The 'savvy' veterans wanted to return to their old units, and commonly went AWOL (Absent Without Leave) to hitch a ride forward – whereupon their old outfits looked the other way and gladly took them in. The fresh replacements were ushered in small groups to their new units, usually in the front line and in the dark. Friendless and almost untrained in surviving this deadly environment, they were killed and wounded in droves, often still anonymous to the GIs of their platoons. In historian Stephen Ambrose's *Citizen Soldier* he says of the 'reppledepple' system: 'Had the Germans been given a free hand to devise a replacement system for the ETO, one that would do the Americans most harm and least good, they could not have done a better job.' General Norman Cota, who distinguished himself in combat as second-in-command of the 29th Division on Omaha beach, considered it both foolish and downright cruel to send a green young man into action in this way, robbed of the psychological support of buddies he had trained with and leaders he knew.

The authorities slowly realised the brutal and wasteful nature of the system, but did little to improve it beyond changing the name 'replacements' to 'reinforcements'. Some divisions took it on themselves to introduce reforms, however; they began holding replacements back after their arrival for (re)training by veteran NCOs. These men were then hopefully introduced to their new units out of the front line, with a chance to get to know, and be known by, their leaders and comrades. These replacements had a much higher survival rate and more quickly became assets to their units.

In addition to some 10,000 or more African-American soldiers of non-combat units who volunteered for infantry service in response to Gen Eisenhower's call during the manpower crisis of winter 1944/45, other classes of recent civilians and soldiers were also rushed forward to swell the ranks of the rifle companies, including deferred college men (ASTP), surplus air cadets, and GIs stripped out of anti-aircraft, tank

March 1945: crossing the Rhine in a DUKW, a lieutenant from an amphibious unit glances back at GIs of the 89th Division. Many seem to be wearing the new two-part M1944 pack system (see Plate G2).

Luxembourg, February 1945: a gunner checks the angle on the barrel of his M12 155mm self-propelled howitzer. These guns were sometimes used, as here, in the direct fire role during serious street and fortress fighting; the effect was devastating.

destroyer, and other support units. These were intelligent and sometimes seasoned men, making the quality of replacements received at the end of the war surprisingly superior.

ARTILLERY

Historically, Americans have been a technically minded people. As early as the 1840s the 'flying artillery' of the Mexican War earned a high reputation, and at most periods, including World War II, the artillery has been the most effective branch in the US Army. The artillery suffered far fewer casualties than the infantry, and this contributed to its level of professionalism and cohesion. The quality of its mostly redesigned and sometimes motorised guns was about average for the period, but US-developed fire control and ammunition made all the difference.

Ammunition was first rate and usually in good supply. By German standards, US employment of artillery was lavish. In part due to its availability, US leaders were much more willing to expend ammunition than men. The introduction of air-bursting VT (radar) ammunition in late 1944 made the US guns even more deadly. With the use of Forward Observers, light spotter aircraft and telephone/radio communications to tie them together at a Fire Direction Center (FDC) they had unequalled potential to co-ordinate their fires, creating a specially devastating 'Time on Target' (ToT) technique. ToT was executed by mathematically co-ordinating different guns at different locations to land their shells on target at exactly the same moment. The FDC's accuracy and speed in calculating the complex mathematics was aided by a US-developed artillery Graphical Firing Table (GFT) slide rule.

105mm howitzer
The war began with the Army using both the old French 75mm howitzer and the newer M5 3in (75mm) gun. By 1943 the 75mm was rapidly disappearing from all but anti-tank work. The M2 105mm howitzer soon became the most common US artillery piece of the war. It had a range of 12,200 yards (11km, 7 miles) and used high explosive (HE), white phosphorus (WP) and smoke ammunition. The towed gun with shield weighed about 2.5 tons; the 75mm and 105mm shared

the same carriage. The 105mm was also mounted as the M7 Priest self-propelled gun, based on an M3 Grant tank hull and weighing about 25 tons. The M7 had a seven-man crew and was also armed with a .50cal machine gun in a kind of forward 'pulpit' – thus its name. It was first issued in 1942 and over 3,000 were ultimately built.

Pack howitzers

The 75mm pack howitzer was developed after World War I as a light field piece that could be broken down and 'packed' by six mules in rough terrain; it was also modified as a horse-drawn weapon. By World War II the 1.1-ton M3 pack howitzer was issued to infantry units to fill out their cannon companies, in which role it was commonly used in the Pacific. An airborne M8 version weighing 1,300lbs (590kg) was parachuted or glidered in for use by the artillery units of the airborne divisions. A larger 105mm pack howitzer weighing 1.3 tons was available by 1944; its accuracy left something to be desired and at 8,300 yards (7.6km, 4.7 miles) its range fell about 1,000 yards short of that of the 75mm. Used in the Pacific, Italy and in airborne operations, the little pack guns did yeoman service.

Heavy artillery

Based on the French 155mm GPF gun, the 155mm gun/howitzer also proved a very successful weapon system. (Note that both the 155mm and 8in artillery pieces came in different 'howitzer' and longer-barrelled, longer-ranging 'gun' versions.) The new M1 155mm howitzer weighed 6.4 tons and its HE, WP and smoke shells had a range of 16,300 yards (14.9km, 9.2 miles). The longer-barrelled M1 155mm gun weighed 15 tons and could fire HE and AP shells over 25,000 yards (22.8km, 14.2 miles). Some of the older M1918A1 155mm guns were mounted on M3 Grant hulls as M12 self-propelled artillery. After limited use in North Africa, six battalions were belatedly fielded in Normandy. It was guessed that the guns would be useful for direct fire operations against fortifications, and indeed they made short work of all but the stoutest, as well as providing general indirect fire support.

Due to availability of British ammunition a 4.5in gun was also built to supplement the 155mm; this was slightly heavier than the 155mm howitzer at 6.6 tons, and its 55lb ammunition did not have the hitting power of the 155mm's 95lb shell. The heavy 8in howitzer shared

Under camouflage netting, gunners of an African-American artillery unit man the standard M2 105mm howitzer during a fire mission; note the locally-cut timber under the wheels. Nine independent black artillery units served in France and Germany, of which the 969th FA Bn (Colored), an VIII Corps outfit equipped with M1A1 155mm howitzers, won a Distinguished Unit Citation for its defence of Bastogne.

the 155mm's gun carriage, weighed about 15 tons and had a range of 18,500 yards (16.8km, 10.5 miles). Independent corps artillery battalions were usually armed with 155mm ('Long Tom'), 4.5in and 8in pieces.

Super-heavy artillery
The 'siege gun' version of the 8in gun weighed 35 tons; used by both the US Navy and Army, it fired shells weighing over 200lbs (90.7kg) to ranges of up to 35,000 yards (32km, 19.8 miles). The GIs learned that if they drilled a small hole through the shell fuze it caused a satisfying screaming sound as the round went down range. The 240mm howitzer weighed 32 tons and could fire its 360lb (163kg) HE round 25,200 yards (22.8km, 14 miles). Both the 240mm howitzer and the 8in gun used a wheelless split trail carriage. They were employed for the first time in the defence of Anzio; these weapons were later transferred to France for use against the fortified port cities.

La Haye du Puits, Normandy, summer 1944: a heavy weapons team from the 79th Division bring up their 81mm mortar. The tube and the baseplate each weighed 45lbs (20kg), and the GIs use shoulder pads to cushion the load. In the left background one man wears the pannier-like ammo vest to carry rounds.

Rockets
Mindful of the success of the Russians and Germans in deploying rocket-propelled 'artillery', the US also fielded rockets in late 1944. The 4.5in finned rocket was used with limited success in saturation bombardment missions. The rockets were mounted on truck beds or on the turrets of some unhappy Sherman tanks (model T34). As the rockets had a large launch signature, it was expedient for rocket units to 'shoot and scoot'.

Anti-tank guns
In 1939 production of the M3 37mm anti-tank gun began; this was generally based on the German 37mm, and over 20,000 were made in 1939–43. This drop-breach gun weighed just over 900lbs (408kg) and was used both as an AT gun and in the M3/M5 Stuart tank series; it could fire HE, AP, and a very useful canister ('grapeshot') round. The

July 1944: in the wrecked streets of St Lô, Normandy, GIs unhitch a 57mm anti-tank gun from a halftrack smothered in their slung packs. This US version of the British 6-pdr AT gun was barely adequate by 1944 standards but was used for lack of anything better.

37mm was adequate for use against Japanese tanks, but by the time of its deployment against the Germans in Tunisia it was ineffective. By 1944 the 37mm was only to be seen in the Pacific and in US light tanks.

The need for a heavier AT gun led to US production of the current British 6-pounder (57mm). The US M1 57mm weighed 2,700 lbs (1225kg) and

fired AP or HE rounds, and

was known for its vicious recoil. Some 16,000 had been made when production ceased in 1944; although it continued in service throughout the war it was obsolete for AT work by that date.

The M5 3in (75mm) artillery piece was used for anti-tank work with good results in Tunisia. With a redesigned gunshield this 2.5-ton piece gave effective service until VE-Day. The M2 90mm AT gun used in the M36 tank destroyer and M26 tank was also built as a split-trail towed AT gun, but none reached combat before VE-Day.

Anti-aircraft guns

The US began the war with the M2 3in AA gun and a new M1 90mm gun. Also quick to come on line was the SCR 268/584 radar fire control system. A M2 90mm gun with gunshield was produced in 1943 which could be used for both AT and AA fire. The combination of radar guidance and the VT fuze made this AA gun extremely effective. The M2 weighed 16 tons and could fire up to 34,000 feet (10,360m, 6 miles). A 120mm AA gun was fielded in 1945 that could fire over 47,000 feet (14,325 meters).

For tactical AA defence both the water- and air-cooled .50cal machine guns were used, as was the M1 US version of the British 40mm Bofors gun. The M16/17 halftrack mounting quadruple .50s in an electrically powered Maxson turret was the most common AA seen at unit level; some 3,500 were built from May 1943. A towed trailer version of the quad mount, and an M15 halftrack with two .50s and one 37mm gun, were less common.

Tactical air support

Air forces naturally tend to see their roles as fighting for air superiority and attacking strategic targets; ground troops are only marginally assisted by such operations. The German *Blitzkrieg* of 1940 had demonstrated that aircraft could also be used as mobile artillery, but the US Army Air Corps was reluctant to be tied down to directly supporting ground actions. This to some extent negated Allied air superiority over the battlefield, and in Tunisia and Sicily it was usually the Luftwaffe that did the strafing and fighterbombing. By 1944 Air Corps Gen Quesada planned to rectify this failure in the ETO by assigning special teams of airmen – including experienced pilots – to accompany spearhead ground units as liaison officers.

The Ninth Air Force had seven tactical fighter bomber groups (each usually of three squadrons) and one photo-recce group, specifically tasked with supporting the ground troops. Each corps, division, armoured combat command and mechanised cavalry group headquarters

Operation Varsity, the Allied airborne crossing of the Rhine in March 1945, saw the first combat use of the 'recoilless rifle'; both the M18 57mm and M20 75mm were issued in limited numbers. Here GIs of the 17th Airborne Division prepare to fire the 57mm weapon, which was found to be an excellent replacement for the 2.36in bazooka; it fired HE and smoke as well as AP rounds. Note that the gunner has sewn a carbine ammo pouch to the sleeve of his M1943 field jacket.

Belgium, winter 1944:
90mm anti-aircraft gunners of the 11th AA Group firing furiously in an attempt to bring down a German V-1 flying bomb on its way to Antwerp or London. Several belts of US and British AA units were set up to try to counter this new threat.

had an AAF radio team; Tactical Air Liaison Officers rode radio-equipped jeeps (and sometimes tanks) with forward units, vectoring the P-47s onto immediate targets just like artillery FOs; ground-fired smoke and WP rounds were also used to mark targets for the aviators. This tighter co-ordination between ground and air became a critical part in the success of US ground operations.

It was also over the objections of the Air Corps that L4 Piper Cub 'Grasshopper' planes were procured for scouting and FO work. By 1944 the co-ordination between the Grasshoppers and the artillery was such that the appearance of this low, slow, flimsy and unarmed light aircraft could paralyse an entire German sector.

ENGINEERS

The combat engineer battalion assigned to each division was an important and valuable asset. They received some of the most rigorous training in the Army. Engineers were generally well armed and provided with .50cal machine guns and flamethrowers as well as mines and explosives. They were responsible for the bulldozers and bridging equipment so vital for breaching obstacles. Considering the multiple skills displayed by the engineers, it was the common GI joke that 'At least they were learning a trade'.

In Normandy, the engineers blasted holes in the massive banked hedgerows and, along with Ordnance, welded the Cullin pronged hedgerow-busting devices to the fronts of tanks. The following winter the 1128th Engineer Combat Group in Bastogne and engineer units throughout the Bulge repeatedly proved themselves key players in delaying and stopping the German spearheads.

The bulldozer was essentially an American invention, and it proved a life-saver in building and maintaining the logistical link between the front lines and the supply depots. In the Pacific it was the 'dozer that created resupply lines and airstrips in the jungles of New Guinea and the Philippines. Some bulldozers were fitted with an armoured cab because of snipers; and for obstacle-clearance under fire 'dozer blades were also fitted to Sherman tanks.

A major mission of the combat engineers was dealing with mines. Both the US anti-tank (M1A1) and anti-personnel mine were considered adequate but under-powered. The Hawkins mine was a light device capable (just) of blowing the track off a tank, and was used primarily by Airborne troops in Normandy. For mine location and lifting the SCR 625 mine detector was used; this could find metal mines buried up to 18 inches deep. It was fragile, however; not waterproof; and required the operator to stand exposed while using it. Probes or bayonets carefully shoved into the earth at a 30-degree angle, by GIs inching forward and making a finger-tip search of the ground ahead, were a common if nerve-racking expedient.

The Japanese rarely used buried mines but the

Mine-clearing, Trier, Germany, March 1945: engineers from the 10th Armored Division pay the price of getting it wrong. The nearer casualty has a chance, and the medics are dressing his badly injured face, left arm and left leg (note that the left-hand medic has his own serial number stencilled on top of his helmet). The casualty lying ignored in the background seems to be dead already from massive head injuries.

Germans frequently employed them. For anti-personnel work the German 'S' mine or 'Bouncing Betty' was commonly encountered; once set off by a 7lb foot pressure the initial charge blew the mine about 4ft into the air before the bursting charge sent the shrapnel filling scything in all directions. The smaller 'Schu' mine was made of wood and thus difficult to detect; its ½lb to 2lb charge was capable of shattering a man's leg and blowing off his foot. The Teller mine was the powerful German anti-tank pattern. Many of these mines were booby-trapped when laid to prevent their extraction. The GIs did not envy the combat engineer his job.

In addition to mine detection, engineers also used explosives themselves. The British-developed 'Bangalore torpedo' was a 5ft long, 2in diameter pipe filled with 8.5lbs of ammonium nitrate explosive. Bangalores were pushed ahead on the surface of the ground to clear obstacles; as well as cutting wire entanglements – their primary purpose – they could set off concealed enemy mines by sympathetic detonation. (A disadvantage was that nearby mines which were not set off by the explosion would commonly become 'tenderised', i.e. very sensitive and hazardous.) Sections of pipe could be fitted together to lengthen the charge; a larger version called a 'snake' was also used. Other explosives used by combat engineers included 'primacord' (detcord), and ½lb or 1lb blocks of TNT.

Bridging was another primary function of engineers. Pneumatic raft pontoon bridges were common, as was the use of the British-developed prefabricated steel girder Bailey bridge with a 40-ton loading capacity (i.e. capable of carrying tanks). The Bailey was quick to put in, but erecting it

was found to be a difficult and dangerous task for the engineers; the US Army was slow to embrace the Bailey, although it revolutionised the deployment of tactical bridges. It should be noted that the Army accepted the Corps of Engineers requirement that tanks have a limited width and weight (30–35 tons) to match existing tactical bridging capacity. This limitation further slowed the development of a heavier modernised tank.

TANKS

The development and characteristics of US tanks in World War II is a vast subject covered in detail in many other publications. The following brief notes are intended only as a very basic introduction.

M4 Sherman

Mine-planting, Hotton, Belgium, December 1944: a GI – probably from the 51st Engineer Combat Battalion, a 1st Army unit operating with Combat Command R of 3rd Armored Division – carefully places an anti-tank mine to slow up the advance of 116th Panzer Division during the German offensive in 'the Bulge'. On 21 December this important bridge over the Ourthe was successfully defended by a scratch force of HQ personnel, engineers and two Sherman tanks. This man wears his cartridge belt hanging open on its suspenders, for comfort.

The majority of US vehicles of the 1940s were gasoline (petrol) powered and mechanically very reliable. Unfortunately, tanks using gasoline (as opposed to diesel fuel) are more likely to burst into flames when hit. The German and British nicknames for the M4 Sherman, 'Tommy Cooker' and 'Ronson' – after a popular brand of cigarette lighter – were significant: over 60 per cent of knocked-out Shermans burned. (The greatest factor in the initial detonation was loose or unprotected stowage of main gun ammunition, however.) Nevertheless, the Sherman series was the best tank available to the Western Allies in early 1942; and faced by the vast task of outfitting not only US but also Allied armies, America kept the Sherman in production throughout the war. It weighed between 30 and 35 tons, mounted a short 75mm gun and two or three machine guns, and had a crew of five; maximum armour thickness was 50mm (hull) and 75mm (turret).

In the constant race with German designers, US tanks rapidly fell behind in both armour protection and main armament. By the time of the Tunisian campaign the Sherman was already being outclassed by the new long 75mm gun mounted in late models of the German PzKw IV, but US tank losses were written off as due to poor training and tactics, soon to be corrected. The Sicilian and southern Italian campaigns saw minimal tank-vs-tank action; and the US Army landed in France in June 1944 expecting the Sherman to do well against the opposition. The actual experience of the crews – at first trapped in the tight country of the Normandy *bocage,* where the defending Germans had all the advantages – soon produced a 'Tiger psychosis'. US tanks were unable to inflict or survive significant damage in straightforward confrontations with the German 75mm PzKw V Panther at most battle ranges, or at virtually any range against the massive 88mm PzKw VI Tiger.

Comparatively speaking, the Allied types were both under-gunned and under-armoured – sometimes chronically so – throughout the war. Thin armour on tank destroyers and Stuart tanks, and barely adequate armour on the Sherman, is evidenced in many photos by the piling of sandbags and extra track plates on the hull fronts. This was nothing more than a 'bandaid' to make the crew feel better; the provision of extra plates welded to the sides over the ammo stowage areas was of more help, as was the water-jacket 'wet stowage' fitted to some Shermans. The M4A3E2 Jumbo which appeared in autumn 1944 was a Sherman with frontal armour protection essentially doubled; placed at the front of tank columns to act as an anti-tank fire 'magnet', it was successful, but only 254 were built.

As well as having guns with about twice the effective range of the US 75mm, the Panther and Tiger were massively armoured. Despite the introduction of the 76mm Sherman in mid-1944, tanks with the new turret only replaced about half of the 75mm Shermans with front-line battalions before VE-Day. The 76mm gun had better armour penetration but a weak HE shell, no WP round, and left room for the stowage of 30 per cent fewer shells. Although some generals – including Patton – were unconvinced of the need for the new gun, after the 76mm Sherman reached the front it was a high-demand item and many 75mm tanks were retrofitted. Units sometimes borrowed the new High Velocity Armor Penetrating (HVAP) ammo or 'hyper-shot' from M18 tank destroyer battalions, giving their 76mm Shermans 50 per cent more penetration at under 500 yards; even so, the 76mm often 'scuffed' rather than penetrated the heavier German tanks. Only the appearance in small numbers of the 90mm M36 tank destroyer in late 1944, and of M26 Pershing tanks in 1945, theoretically gave American tankers the edge. However, other factors outweighed the bare mathematics of armour thickness and gun power.

US tanks had speed, mechanical reliability, radio co-ordination, fast gun loading and turret speed on their side – as well as sheer numbers in the field. Centrally, the decision to standardise the versatile M3, M4 and M10 hulls, drive trains and suspensions also gave US Ordnance a huge edge in ease and speed of manufacturing; large numbers of variant models, from self-propelled artillery to armoured recovery vehicles, were produced on these basic chassis. The US production of Shermans alone – 57,000 by July 1945 – represented twice the total tank production of Germany and Britain combined.

Luckily, there were never very many Panthers or more than a handful of Tigers on the battlefield. US armour commanders adapted by bringing the co-ordination of superior numbers, artillery and airpower to an unequalled level as a 'force multiplier'. The provision of good

October 1944: M4 Sherman medium tank of the 32nd or 33rd Armored Regiment, 3rd Armored Division, giving a ride to GIs of the division's 36th Armored Infantry Regiment. Note the extra plate commonly welded on the hull over the ammo stowage area inside. The stack of sandbags on the front might help protect against the contact-detonated *Panzerfaust* used by German infantry, but were of no practical use against the AP shot of tanks and anti-tank guns.

US armoured divisions were configured into three fighting brigades or 'combat commands' (CCA, CCB, and CCR). Combat Commands A and B were fluid organisations embracing various infantry, tank and artillery units and attachments as the mission required. Combat Command R (for Reserve) was commonly the smallest CC and usually composed of resting or left-over units.

Germany, 1945: in the streets of a captured town a GI – apparently wearing a Parsons jacket over winter overalls – poses for an Army photographer in front of an M5A1 Stuart light tank. Note the 'duckbill' extensions to widen the track and give better floatation on soft ground – this was also a problem for the M4 Sherman. By the time of the November 1942 Operation Torch landings in North Africa the Stuart was already completely out-gunned and under-armoured for combat against Panzers, but it served on until 1945 in the reconnaissance role.

radio communications should not be underestimated as a factor in this success: every US tank had a receiver (SCR 538), and leaders' tanks – and by 1945 most others – had transmitters and receivers (SCR 508/528). The Sherman platoons manoeuvred to ambush the Panzers, fired WP rounds to blind the enemy, flank- or back-shooting them from short range, playing cat and mouse in cover, and relying on speed and numbers in break-through battles to make the most of their equipment. It is a tribute to the American crews that they were able to fight the US tanks through the 1944/45 ETO campaign and win essentially every major battle. After the German retreat from France in late summer 1944 there was a steady shift, in the US Army's favour, in the level of skills shown by German versus American tank crews.

Most US tanks were given standard model designations, e.g. M4 Medium. The British, who were heavy users of US tanks, had a tradition of naming the types, and gave them American generals' names – Stuart for the M3 Light, Grant and Lee for different versions of the M3 Medium, and Sherman for the M4 Medium. The GIs adopted most of these names, and the Army began officially naming tank models by the end of the war. The crews commonly grew attached to their vehicles and sometimes named them individually, usually using the initial letter of their company (i.e., B Co – Betty, Barbara, Beauty, etc).

M26 Pershing

Development of the M26 Pershing heavy tank was suddenly given high priority in autumn 1944. Weighing 46 tons and mounting a 90mm M3 gun, it was capable of knocking out most German tanks. The Pershing began arriving at the front by February 1945, the 3rd and 9th Armored Divisions receiving the first limited issue. By VE-Day, of the 700 built, 310 were in the ETO and 200 of these were in combat units. Some M26s arrived in Okinawa in August 1945 too late to see use.

M3/M5 Stuart series

The US Army fought in Tunisia with both the M3 and improved M5 Stuart 16-ton light tank. Armed with an M6 37mm main gun and the

VEHICLE MARKINGS
For identification purposes US vehicles were usually marked with prominent white stars; each theatre of operations had its own variation as to how these were to be applied. By 1944, GIs believed the stars, stripes and rings were too high profile and gave the enemy an aiming point, so these markings were commonly dirtied, reduced or painted over. For identification from the air high visibility coloured and shaped recognition panels and flags were used.

A semi-standardised system of unit number/letter bumper/hull markings was developed, using flat white stencilling. The standard order, seen from left to right facing the vehicle, was division-regiment-company-vehicle; the company letter and vehicle number were usually separated from the divisional and unit numbers. Armies used an 'A', artillery used 'F' or 'FA', infantry used 'I', Airborne used 'AB', headquarters used 'HQ', TDs used 'TD' and Armored units used a triangle. Thus e.g.:
75I-291I B6 would identify 75th Infantry Division, 291st Infantry Regiment, B Company, vehicle 6; and
82AB-505AB A2 identified 82nd Airborne Division, 505th Parachute Infantry Regiment, A Company, vehicle 2.

Ardennes, January 1945: two GIs from the 84th Division (note the medic's 'Railsplitters' shoulder patch) link up with a whitewashed M8 Greyhound from the 11th Armored Division. This six-wheeled armoured car mounted a 37mm M6 gun in an open-topped turret and two machine guns, had a four-man crew, and weighed just under nine tons. The M20, essentially a turretless M8 with a .50cal MG on a ring mount, was used as a scout vehicle and command car. The armour gave protection against small arms fire only, but with its high road speed of up to 55mph the Greyhound was widely used in mechanised cavalry units.

Within infantry divisions the company-strength reconnaissance and screening units were designated Cavalry Reconnaissance Troops; they operated with 18 jeeps and 12 M8 Greyhounds. In armoured divisions there was a Cavalry Reconnaissance Squadron (or Battalion). This 900-plus strong unit had three recon troops (or companies); a light tank troop with 17 M5s or M24s; and an assault gun troop of six M8 75mm Howitzer Motor Carriages. The largest cavalry unit was the Group, made up of two squadrons; commanded by a full colonel, one was usually assigned per corps. Patton's 3rd Army had the 6th Cavalry Group ('Patton's Household Cavalry') specially configured with radios reporting directly to his HQ.

usual coaxial, hull front and turret-top machine guns, the slab-sided little Stuart had a crew of four. By the time production stopped in 1944 the Stuart was dangerously out of date, though still employed in reconnaissance units, where its crews depended for their lives on its high speed and excellent manoeuvrability.

M24 Chaffee

The 20-ton M24, named after Gen Adna Chaffee, was the best light tank produced during the war; it began to replace the Stuart in the ETO from November 1944. Mounting the M6 75mm gun, which used Sherman ammo, the four-man M24 had lighter but much better sloped armour than the archaic-looking M5. It was powered by two V8s from the Stuart, used Hellcat suspension, and had a top speed of 35mph.

TANK DESTROYERS

The M3 halftrack with a 75mm howitzer was the first mobile TD available, seeing service in North Africa and Sicily as a temporary expedient. The low velocity gun lacked penetration and had a very limited traverse, and GIs found that firing at the wrong angle could cause the track to fall over. The M3 was soon replaced with the M10.

All the thinly armoured TDs had open-top turrets, which allowed better visibility and elbow room to load quickly. Unfortunately, they also exposed the five-man crew to artillery fire and close assault by enemy infantry. TDs were not solely employed as anti-tank guns but could also be committed in general support of infantry, for 'bunker-busting', and dug in hull-down as field artillery The Tank Destroyer Battalion fielded 36 TDs in three companies, plus an HQ Co with six short-barrelled 75mm M8 HMCs. The US Army formed 71 TD battalions, both self-propelled and towed, and 61 of these served in the ETO/MTO. Due

to their specialised anti-tank mission GIs referred to the TDs as 'can openers'. The TD concept was abandoned and units were disbanded in 1946.

M10 Wolverine

The M10 was the first TD vehicle specially designed for the AT mission. It mounted the M7 3in (75mm) naval gun, which could penetrate 3ins of steel at 1,000 yards – a more powerful weapon than the M3 75mm of the Sherman. The gun could fire HE, AP, canister and smoke. More than 7,000 of this 33-ton vehicle had been built when production stopped in late 1943. The workhorse of the TD units, it saw action in North Africa, Italy and throughout the ETO, and to a limited extent in the Pacific.

Germany, February 1945: beside a pile of discarded cardboard ammo packing tubes, a 75mm M8 HMC of an assault gun troop from 106th Cavalry Group lays down fire. Based on the M3/M5 Stuart hull, the open-topped M8 was assigned in small numbers to both recon units and tank unit HQ elements to deliver direct and indirect HE fire. Limited, but well liked, the M8 was replaced in 1945 by a 105mm howitzer Sherman which offered more punch and better protection.

M18 Hellcat

The M18 featured the same M1 76mm gun used by the up-graded Sherman, but Hellcat crews also had the use of effective High Velocity Armor Piercing ammunition with a tungsten carbide core. Over 2,500 M18s had been built when production ceased in late 1944. This 20-ton vehicle had a powerful 400hp engine, which could propel it at speeds in excess of 45mph. With its outstanding power/weight ratio and good gun, the M18 was the most effective US TD of the war, and the GIs loved it.

M36 Jackson

Over 1,100 M36s were produced by retrofitting existing M10s with the powerful M3 90mm gun also used on the Pershing tank; interestingly, at 31 tons it weighed less than the M10. The first models reached the Normandy front in July 1944; offering a good chance of destroying Panthers and Tigers even at long range, the M36 finally gave the GIs something like an equal chance against the late model Panzers.

M10 Wolverine of a tank destroyer battalion, fitted with the 'Cullin device' for tearing a way through the massively banked hedgerows of Normandy. Again, note the piled sandbags; the M10's thin armour was no match for the main armament of the Panzers by 1944, and a single layer of sandbags was not going to help. Exposed by their open-top turret, the crew wear M1 steel helmets against the shrapnel of enemy air-bursts.

ENGLAND, 1944
1: Colonel, Corps of Engineers, US 3rd Army
2: Captain, 70th Tank Battalion
3: Platoon Sgt, 66th Armd Regt, 2nd Armored Division

A

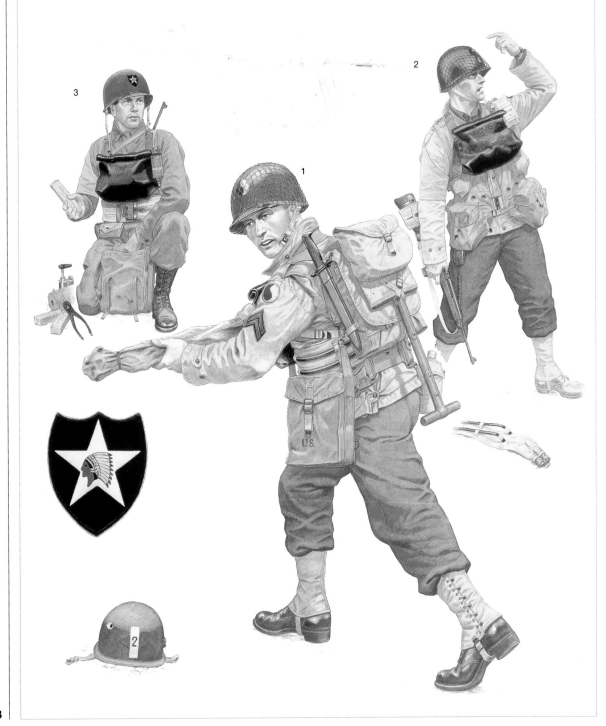

OMAHA BEACH, 6 JUNE 1944
1: Corporal, 116th Inf Regt, 29th Infantry Division
2: 1st Lieutenant, 116th Inf Regt, 29th Inf Div
3: T/5, Engineers, 2nd Infantry Division

B

OPERATION COBRA, NORMANDY, JULY 1944
1: Rifleman, 41st Armd Inf Regt, 2nd Armored Division
2: BAR gunner, 8th Inf Regt, 4th Infantry Division
3: Rifleman, 41st Armd Inf Regt, 2nd Armored Division

FRANCE, 1944
1: Corporal, Women's Army Corps, SHAEF
2: Sergeant, 104th Inf Regt, 26th Inf Div
3: Captain, 761st Tank Bn (Colored)

D

NETHERLANDS, OCTOBER 1944
1: Major, 23rd Armd Inf Regt, 7th Armored Div
2: Pfc radio operator, 23rd Armd Inf Regt, 7th Armd Div
3: Captain, Forward Air Controller, 9th Air Force

E

BASTOGNE, DECEMBER 1944
1: Rifleman, 28th Infantry Division
2: Bazooka gunner, 327th Glider Inf Regt,
   101st Airborne Division
3: T/5, 20th Armd Inf Regt,
   10th Armored Division

1

2

3

F

GERMANY, SPRING 1945
1: 2nd Lieutenant, Army Nurse Corps
2: Rifleman, 89th Infantry Division
3: Medic, 45th Infantry Division

ARMY OF OCCUPATION, 1945
1: WO glider pilot, 61st Troop Carrier Gp, 9th Air Force
2: T/5, 505th Parachute Inf Regt, 82nd Airborne Division
3: 1st Sergeant, 26th Inf Regt, 1st Infantry Division

H

Tank destroyer doctrine

The shocking success of the German 1940 *Blitzkrieg* galvanised the US Army into planning a response. Liberally deployed anti-tank guns would theoretically hold enemy tanks in check, and wargames conducted in 1941 seemed to confirm this hypothesis. The doctrine evolved by the Army called for tank destroyer (TD) units to deal with enemy tanks while US tanks were used to support the infantry and serve as an exploitation force. Towed 37mm and 57mm AT guns were assigned to divisions and TD battalions; and the 75mm howitzer was expediently mounted on halftracks to increase mobility until the M10 TD arrived in sufficient numbers to serve as the self-propelled AT weapons platform.

The new TD doctrine was to play a key role in retarding the possible up-grades of the M4 Sherman; this tank was seen by the Ordnance theorists and by many generals as an infantry support and exploitation vehicle rather than a tank-killer. Thus offers by the Ordnance in 1943 to up-gun the M4 to 76mm or 90mm were refused as 'overkill'; up-grading the armour also seemed unnecessary, as the tank was supposed to manoeuvre around enemy tanks or wait for the TDs to deal with the problem.

The TD doctrine also influenced how the Army organised its divisions for combat. The majority of the numbered Tank Battalions and all the TD Battalions were to be independent units assigned at corps level, and deployed as the situation demanded. Infantry divisions had no integral tanks and only a handful of towed AT guns. Armoured divisions alone had integral tank units, as they were by nature break-through formations. Tank and especially TD battalions were usually farmed out within a division by companies or platoons; the TD group and battalion HQs were commonly redundant. The ETO solution was to all but permanently assign independent tank and TD battalions to the infantry divisions.

However well thought out this doctrine may have been, it did not seem to work. TD units were never numerous enough to cover where required, and were commonly undergunned. Their open-top turrets made them vulnerable to field artillery. The M10 and M36 were so thinly armoured that they could not stand in the open or advance and fight; they had to be very carefully handled, using 'bushwhacking' techniques to be most effective. Desperate commanders were forced to use the Sherman (sometimes suicidally mismatched) to stop enemy tank thrusts. Though TD units had been used with limited success in 1943, their reverses had been blamed on faulty deployment and shortages of the new M10. After D-Day the generals finally acknowledged the bankrupt

Near Bitburg, Germany, 1945: GIs from the 4th Armored Division cross the undefended 'dragon's-teeth' of a pacified section of the Siegfried Line. Note the two medics (centre) with unusual helmet markings showing the red cross with only a thin white edge; the radioman with an SCR 300 and accessory pack; and the use of gasmask bags as haversacks (see Plate G2).

nature of the TD doctrine. This resulted in a belated concentration on the development of new tanks, like the M26 Pershing, serious enough to take on the German Panthers and Tigers.

The mismatch between German and US tanks is typified by the mid-November 1944 engagement between the US 2nd Armored and German 9th Panzer divisions at Pfuffendorf in Germany. Without air support and with no room to manoeuvre, two battalions of 75mm and 76mm Shermans (100-plus tanks) from the 67th Armd Regt were forced to fight just 20–25 PzKw IVs, Panthers and Tigers in a frontal engagement. To have a chance, the M4s tried to close to bring their guns into effective range. One 76mm Sherman fired 14 rounds into a Tiger before disabling it, and was immediately destroyed by the 88mm gun of another Tiger. The 67th Armor claimed five German tanks destroyed for the day; the timely arrival of the 90mm M36s of the 702nd TD Bn cost the Germans 15 more tanks; but the 67th lost 38 M4s, 19 M5s, and over 350 men in this engagement.

ETO CAMPAIGN SUMMARY

The Normandy landings

During the early morning of D-Day, 6 June 1944, some 2,500 bombers and 600 warships pounded the German 'Atlantic Wall' defences on the coast of Normandy between the Vire and Orne river estuaries (most of the bombardment falling too far inland to be of much value). Operation Overlord, under the supreme command of Gen Dwight Eisenhower, put three British and Canadian divisions ashore on 'Gold', 'Juno' and 'Sword' beaches at the eastern end of the 50-mile stretch, with British 6th Airborne Division dropped by night to secure the flank and bridges inland. The US 82nd and 101st Airborne Divisions were night-dropped behind the beaches designated for the US 1st Army (Gen Omar Bradley); despite bad scattering they secured vital road junctions and interdicted enemy reinforcements. To the west, the US 4th Infantry Division landed on 'Utah' beach at the base of the Cotentin peninsula, losing less than 200 men. On 'Omaha', about 11 miles further east, the 1st and 29th Infantry Divisions, 2nd and 5th Rangers were stopped cold on the beach, suffering more than 2,000 casualties – 50 to 95 per cent in some assault units. A handful of squads and platoons led by every rank from private to

Normandy, summer 1944: two medics and a rifleman from the 35th Division examine a dead German. The rifleman (left) has sawn off his E-tool handle for ease of carrying; his 'beer gut' is probably ammo and rations stuffed into his field jacket to save wearing a pack. Note that the kneeling medic has a second red cross brassard attached to his helmet net – a not uncommon sight. The medic partly visible in the background has turned his Parsons jacket inside-out to show the darker wool lining rather than the more visible light duck exterior.

brigadier-general eventually forced their way up the bluffs, attacking German positions from the flanks and rear until the main beach exit points were cleared; and the two savaged divisions lurched forward into Normandy. By nightfall somewhere between 150,000 and 175,000 Allied troops were ashore in France.

Over the next three days the 2nd Infantry and 2nd Armored Divisions were landed into the slowly expanding bridgehead; soon a new division was landed about every two days. The Cotentin was cut off by 18 June; Cherbourg – a priority objective – fell after a five-day defence on 27 June but the harbour was not fully operational until 7 August.

Operation Cobra

Penned into the narrow bridgehead and taking heavy casualties, the Allies needed to break out of the difficult *bocage* countryside – of small fields bordered by massive hedgerows and sunken lanes – in order to make full use of their superiority in numbers, firepower and mobility. Repeated and costly British and Canadian attempts to take Caen, the eastern anchor of the German defence, did not succeed until 9 July, but did draw the weight of German armoured forces into their sector. To the west the strategic town of St Lô fell to the 29th Infantry Division on 18 July. Operation Cobra, the US break-out assault west of St Lô, was preceded by aerial 'carpet bombing', which obliterated the defending Panzer-Lehr Division (but also killed some 500 US troops of the 30th Infantry Division, and the visiting LtGen McNair). The Americans poured through the breach, seizing Coutances on 28 July and Avranches on the 31st. The US 3rd Army (Gen George Patton), activated on 1 August, swept into Brittany. Hoping to break the neck of the US advance, Hitler ordered his available Panzer forces to attack at Mortain on 6 August. One battalion of the 30th Infantry Division lost about half its men holding Hill 317, but its FOs called down aircraft and corps artillery fires; supported by the 9th and 4th Infantry Divisions, the 30th lost little ground, and the mauled Germans were forced back. Despite this dangerous attack the Allies continued their rapid exploitation attack into France.

Hürtgen Forest, October/ November 1944: a BAR team from the 4th Division struggle through the muddy pine woods. During weeks of murderous fighting GIs from the 4th, 8th and 28th Divisions were among those who paid very dearly for the 1st Army's slow advance.

The battle for France

By mid-August 1944 an opportunity appeared to cut off German forces near Falaise; at first thinking most of the enemy had withdrawn, the Allies were slow to seal off this pocket, but even so Falaise cost the Wehrmacht some 50,000 men and thousands of vehicles and guns. While the British and Canadians advanced along the Channel coast the US 1st and 3rd Armies began to race eastwards across France; the Seine was crossed on 24 August and Paris fell on the 25th. Another 25,000 Germans surrendered near Mons, Belgium, on 3 September; by D+90 days the Allies were occupying objectives that had been planned for D+340. On 11 September, Patton's 3rd Army linked up with Gen Patch's 7th Army advancing from the landings in the south of France on 15 August (Operation Anvil), and a unified Allied front faced the Germans from the Channel to the Mediterranean.

However, the advance now began to sputter to a halt, caused not by German resistance but by over-stretched Allied supply lines from Normandy. The situation got worse when the British received priority of supply to support their attempts on the vital port of Antwerp and the airborne seizure of the lower Rhine (Operation Market Garden – in which ultimately failed gamble both US airborne divisions participated). By the end of October 1944 the 1st Army had captured its first German city, Aachen (21 October), and several toehold breaches were made in the Siegfried Line, the German border defences. In the nearby Hürtgen Forest the US Army allowed three divisions in succession to be ground up by the stubborn defenders. Still begging in vain for sufficient fuel and ammunition supplies, the US armies only slowly consolidated their advance. This autumn pause, called by the Germans the 'Miracle in the West', gave the enemy time to build and re-equip units for the defence of the Reich.

The Battle of the Bulge

Hitler gambled his reconstituted divisions in an all-out offensive to split the US and British armies apart and seize Antwerp. There was little warning of the Wehrmacht's renewed strength until US forces resting in the thinly-held Ardennes sector found themselves under massive attack on 16 December.

Winter weather grounded the Air Corps, leaving three US divisions to face the onslaught; the green 106th, the 28th (recovering from the Hürtgen battles), and parts of the untried 9th Armored held the line for two days under attack by three German armies. The north (2nd and 99th Infantry Divisions) and south (4th Infantry Division) shoulders of the penetration held firm. The shocked 106th Infantry Division ultimately surrendered two of its three regiments; the 28th, fighting stubborn rearguard actions, found its units scattered. US engineer units plagued German spearheads throughout the battle with blown bridges, which caused major delays in the difficult hill country. A 40-mile breach seemed to open, but the two-day stand allowed the highly mobile US Army to rush units into the 'Bulge'.

The Germans had to capture the road junctions at St Vith and Bastogne. With elements of three divisions, Gen Clarke (CCB, 7th Armored

Division) held St Vith until 20 December, completely disrupting the German timetable in the northern Ardennes. When it fell, outflanked by the crack Führer Begleit Brigade, the 7th and nearby 9th Armored Division combat commands managed to break out to fight another day. Bastogne was held by the 101st Airborne and elements of three other divisions. The deepest enemy penetrations, by 1st SS Panzer and 2nd Panzer divisions, were both stopped cold short of the River Meuse. By the end of December encircled Bastogne had been relieved by Patton's 4th Armored Division, and the clearing skies were full of Allied aircraft. Though the German offensive had severely shocked the Allies, Hitler had expended his last reserves for nothing.

The battle for Germany

Spring 1945 saw the US armies careering into the heartland of Germany. In late March the Rhine was jumped at several locations and the 9th Armored Division seized an intact bridge at Remagen. Rapid advances were punctuated by many bitter local battles, however, as US columns encountered blocking positions held with fanatical determination by *ad hoc* German battle groups – always a strength of the German forces: a few tanks and Flak guns, the scraped-together remnants of retreating units, the staffs of officer and NCO training schools, banding together under some junior commander to sell their lives dearly. Nevertheless, by 18 April nearly 400,000 enemy troops were cut off and forced to capitulate in the Ruhr valley, the bombed-out industrial heart of Germany. While fighting doggedly against the vengeful Red Army advancing from the east, most Wehrmacht troops were now happy to surrender to the Western Allies.

By VE-Day the US had 60 divisions operational in the ETO; they were advancing into Austria and Czechoslovakia, and in Germany they were a day's march from Berlin. On 2 May, American, British and Russian troops linked up at Lübeck on the Baltic. On the 7th, the unconditional surrender of Germany from midnight on 8 May 1945 was signed at Gen Eisenhower's HQ at Rheims.

Going home

The GI of World War II has accurately been described as the 'citizen soldier'; and when the war ended he couldn't wait to get home. Conscious of the US Army's unhappy experience with delays in sending the 'doughboys' of 1918 back to the States, the authorities took surveys among the GIs as to the fairest way to handle the problem. A point system was devised to award the longer-serving veterans higher scores which would enable them to go home first: five points for each campaign star, one for every six months in service, one for every six months overseas, five for each wound, five for each decoration, and twelve points for each child (to a maximum of three). The total points required for release started at 85, but by December 1945 only 50 were needed.

After VE-Day priority was given to transferring the newer ETO divisions to the Pacific to continue the war. As VJ-Day in August 1945 caught the Army in mid-transit, many GIs with minimal service found themselves in the US and were discharged. High-point veterans in the ETO were soon first on the list homeward, but it all seemed to the GIs to take entirely too much time. The US Army demobilised at a rapid rate, however, and by 1946 the wartime force of 8.3 million was down to 2 million.

Note: Divisions which served in both Italy and NW Europe are covered in the table at the end of the Mediterranean section: 1st, 3rd, 9th, 36th & 45th Infantry, and 82nd Airborne.

 2nd Armored Division ('Hell on Wheels'). N.Africa, Sicily, Normandy, France, Ardennes, Germany.
All armored divisions wore the Armored Force triangular patch divided yellow (top), blue (left) and red, with black tracks-and-lightning motif below divisional numeral.

 3rd Armored Division ('Spearhead'). Normandy, France, Ardennes, Germany.

 4th Armored Division ('Breakthrough'). Normandy, France, Ardennes, Germany.

 5th Armored Division ('Victory'). Normandy, France, Germany.

 6th Armored Division ('Super Sixth'). Normandy, France, Ardennes, Germany.

 7th Armored Division ('Lucky Seventh'). Normandy, France, Ardennes, Germany.

 8th Armored Division ('Thundering Herd'). France, Ardennes, Germany.

 9th Armored Division ('Phantom'). Ardennes, Germany, Czechoslovakian border.

 10th Armored Division ('Tiger'). France, Ardennes, Germany.

 11th Armored Division ('Thunderbolt'). France, Ardennes, Germany.

 12th Armored Division ('Hellcat'). Germany.

 13th Armored Division ('Black Cat'). Ardennes, Germany.

 14th Armored Division ('Liberator'). France, Germany.

 16th Armored Division Germany.

 20th Armored Division Germany.

 2nd Infantry Division ('Indian Head'). Normandy, France, Ardennes, Leipzig (Germany). Full-colour Indian's head in blue warbonnet on white star on black shield.

 4th Infantry Division ('Ivy'). Normandy, France, Bastogne (Ardennes), Germany. Four conjoined green ivy leaves on khaki diamond.

 5th Infantry Division ('Red Diamond'). Normandy, Metz (France), Ardennes, Mainz-Worms Bridgehead (Germany). Red diamond.

 8th Infantry Division ('Pathfinder'). Normandy, Brittany, France, Ardennes, Cologne (Germany). Yellow arrow through white 8 on blue shield.

 17th Airborne Division ('Golden Talon'). Ardennes, Rhine crossing, Germany. Yellow eagle's talon on black disc edged khaki, below yellow-on-black 'Airborne' tab.

 26th Infantry Division ('Yankee'). France, Ardennes, Siegried Line (Germany). Dark blue 'YD' monogram on khaki diamond.

 28th Infantry Division ('Keystone'). Normandy, Colmar Pocket (France), Hürtgen Forest, Ardennes, Germany. Red keystone shape.

 29th Infantry Division ('Blue & Grey'). Normandy, France, Siegfried Line, Aachen (Germany). Dark blue/grey 'yin & yang'.

 30th Infantry Division ('Old Hickory'). Normandy, France, Ardennes, Germany. Blue 'H' and 'XXX' on red oval edged blue.

 35th Infantry Division ('Santa Fe'). Normandy, Metz, Nancy (France), Ardennes, Ruhr (Germany). White crosses and circle on dark blue disc.

 42nd Infantry Division ('Rainbow'). Schweinfurt, Munich, Dachau (Germany). Quadrant of red, yellow, blue rainbow.

 44th Infantry Division ('Two Fours'). Saar, Ulm (Germany), Danube River. Blue opposed 4s on yellow disc edged blue.

 63rd Infantry Division ('Blood & Fire'). Bavaria (Germany), Danube River. Yellow bayonet, red flames and blood, on khaki teardrop.

 65th Infantry Division ('Battle Axe'). Saarlautern, Regensburg (Germany), Danube River. White halberd on blue shield.

 66th Infantry Division ('Black Panther'). Lorient, St Nazaire (France), Germany. Black panther head, red & white details, on orange disc edged red.

 69th Infantry Division ('Fighting 69th'). Germany. Interlocked, stylised red '6' & blue '9' edged white.

 70th Infantry Division ('Trailblazer'). Saarbrücken, Moselle River (Germany). White axehead & mountain, green trees, on red background.

 71st Infantry Division ('Red Circle'). Hartz Mountains (Germany). Blue stylised '71' on white disc edged red.

 75th Infantry Division Ardennes, Westphalia (Germany). Blue '7' & red '5' on red\white\blue shield.

 76th Infantry Division ('Onaway'). Luxembourg, Germany. White heraldic label on blue over red shield, narrow green divider.

78th Infantry Division ('Lightning'). Aachen, Roer River, Ruhr (Germany). White lightning on red semicircle.

79th Infantry Division ('Lorraine'). Normandy, Vosges Mountains (France), Germany. Grey Cross of Lorraine on blue shield edged grey.

80th Infantry Division ('Blue Ridge'). Normandy, France, relief of Bastogne (Ardennes), Moselle River, Germany.

83rd Infantry Division ('Ohio', 'Thunderbolts'). Normandy, France, Ardennes, Germany. Yellow 'Ohio' monogram on black triangle.

84th Infantry Division ('Railsplitters'). Ardennes, Hanover (Germany).
First: red axe head, blue handle & lettering 'Lincoln' & '84' on white disc edged red.

Second: White axe splitting white log on red disc.

86th Infantry Division ('Black Hawk'). Dachau, Ingolstadt (Germany). Black hawk & 'BH' on red shields.

87th Infantry Division ('Acorn'). Ardennes, Germany, Czechoslovakian border. Yellow acorn on green disc.

89th Infantry Division ('Middle West', 'Rolling W'). Bingen, Eisenach (Germany). Black stylised 'W' and edge on brown disc.

90th Infantry Division ('Texas/Oklahoma', 'Tough Ombres'). Normandy, France, Ardennes, Germany, Czechoslovakian border. Stylised red 'TO' monogram on brown square.

94th Infantry Division ('Neuf Quatres'). St Nazaire (France), Siegried Line, Moselle River, Saar (Germany). Black '9' & khaki '4' on opposite-coloured divided disc.

95th Infantry Division ('Victory'). Metz (France), Moselle River, Siegried Line, Saar (Germany). Red '9' & white 'V' interlaced on blue oval.

97th Infantry Division ('Trident'). Germany. White trident on blue shield edged white.

99th Infantry Division ('Checkerboard'). Ardennes, Remagen Bridgehead (Germany). Blue/white checks on black shield.

100th Infantry Division ('Century'). France, Remagen Bridgehead, Saar (Germany). '100' halved white over yellow, on blue shield.

101st Airborne Division ('Screaming Eagles'). Normandy, Netherlands, Bastogne (Ardennes), Germany. White eagle's head with yellow & red details on black shield under yellow-on-black 'Airborne' tab.

102nd Infantry Division ('Ozark'). Siegfried Line, Ruhr, München-Gladbach (Germany). Yellow overlaid 'O', 'U' & 'Z' on blue disc.

103rd Infantry Division ('Cactus'). Stuttgart (Germany), Austria. Green cactus, blue ground, yellow sky.

104th Infantry Division ('Timberwolves'). Rhine crossing, Cologne, Ruhr (Germany). Grey wolf head on green disc.

106th Infantry Division ('Golden Lions'). St Vith (Ardennes), Germany. Yellow lion mask, red & blue details, on blue disc edged white inside red.

Aboard ship off Normandy, June 1944: this 2nd Division MP checking the Army's official phrase book/travel guide displays the 'Indianhead' patch on his left shoulder and – just visible – painted above the 'MP' on his helmet.

St Vith, Belgium, December
1944: GIs from the 23rd Armored
Infantry, 7th Armored Division
take a watchful rest in the
streets, covered by a whitewashed M4 Sherman. The GIs
are wearing field-expedient
white helmet covers and capes
apparently made from bedsheets.

THE PLATES: NW EUROPE

A: ENGLAND, 1944

A1: Colonel, Corps of Engineers, US 3rd Army

This 'bird' colonel wears his rank on the epaulettes of the regulation officers' service coat in the darker OD shade 51, with trousers of the optional light drab colour popularly known as 'pinks' – in this case with a cavalry-style inseam. Either cap could be worn with this uniform; he has the service cap, in this case an example with a noticeably lighter shade ribbed band – colours varied in officers' privately purchased uniforms. It has the standard russet leather visor and strap and gilt officers' badge. The coat has the drab-on-drab lace band above each cuff indicating officer rank, and – a peculiarity which survives to this day – special Corps of Engineers buttons. Officers' collar badges came in cut-out pairs, here two 'US' cyphers over two Engineer castle emblems. His left chest displays ribbons for service dating back to World War I; among his 'fruit salad' are the DSC and Silver Star, 1918 Victory medal with two campaign/battle stars, the French Croix de Guerre, and both the Pacific and European theatre ribbons. His cuff stripes show one year's overseas service in World War I and two years (four bars) in World War II. Re-enlistment stripes are not worn – officers don't enlist. The 3rd Army patch of an 'A' inside an 'O' represents its service after World War I as the AEF Army of Occupation in Germany.

A2: Captain, 70th Tank Battalion

He chooses to wear a khaki shirt and prewar black tie with his service uniform. The Sam Browne officers' belt, with sword hanger, had been required before the war, but purchase became optional during hostilities. Note the Armored branch emblems on his lower collar, shaped like a British World War I tank. Unit crests for officers, when available, were worn on the epaulettes. This officer wears American Service and ETO ribbons. Independent tank units – i.e. those unassigned to a division – used the Armored Force shoulder patch with no number in the yellow segment; battalion numbers were sometimes custom-woven onto the patches later in the war. The 70th Tank Bn was the first of these independent battalions to be raised, from a picked group of men; it fought in North Africa, Sicily, Normandy, France, the Bulge and Germany. Over his arm this officer carries a trenchcoat; these were to be seen in colours

ranging from khaki-beige to medium green. Originating with the Duke of Wellington's prejudice against officers with umbrellas, it is to this day against regulations for an American officer to carry one (unless with a lady).

A3: Platoon sergeant, 66th Armored Regiment, 2nd Armored Division

This technical or platoon sergeant wears the enlisted man's M1939 four-pocket coat in OD shade 54; either this overseas cap or the limited-issue visored service dress cap ('saucer hat') could be worn with this uniform. The overseas cap could be piped in his mixed green/white arm-of-service colour; it is worn here unpiped but displaying the divisional sign in enamelled metal. On his upper collar are bronze discs bearing the national cypher (right) and his arm-of-service emblem (left). Most GIs did not have pairs of unit crests in enamelled metal for wear on the lower collar, but this NCO proudly wears those of the 66th Armored Regiment. This was the oldest tank unit in the US Army, tracing its roots back to the 351st Tank Battalion in World War I. He wears the divisional patch on his left shoulder, and rank chevrons – in prewar silver-on-black – on both upper sleeves. The two bars on his left forearm are two six-month overseas service stripes (nicknamed 'Hersey bars', after the director of the US Draft, Gen Lewis B.Hersey); the diagonal bar is a re-enlistment stripe, showing this NCO to be a prewar volunteer regular rather than a draftee. On his left chest are the ribbons of the American Service and European-African-Middle Eastern medals, the latter with a bronze campaign star; this NCO fought in Sicily.

August 1944: soldier of the 26th Infantry, 1st Division, wearing the experimental load-carrying combat vest issued in some numbers to assault units of the 1st and 29th Divisions and Rangers for the D-Day landings, but not usually kept this long. On the Normandy beaches the pockets scooped up large quantities of water and wet sand; most GIs found it bulky, hot, burdensome and awkward, and soon discarded it or cut it down. Based on the British limited issue 'battle jerkin' – which the Tommies also disliked – the US cotton duck canvas version had four generous patch pockets on the front and a integral pack and 'butt pack' on the back; the side of the pack had a sleeve for the bayonet, and the shoulders had quick release straps. The vest was closed with buckled web straps at the waist and chest. Normal web belts were supposed to be worn under the vest – not over it, as here – so that it could be shed quickly in the water if necessary. (See Plate B2.)

B: OMAHA BEACH, D-DAY
B1: Corporal, 116th Infantry Regiment, 29th Infantry Division
At H-Hour of D-Day, 6 June 1944, elements of the 1st and 29th Infantry Divisions were the first units to land on Omaha beach, supported by engineer troops and men from the Ranger force. Expecting heavy losses, most D-Day units were 10 per cent overstrength when they embarked. The assaulting regiments of the 29th Division lost about 60 per cent of their men on 6 June.

This corporal wears the 'M1941' Parsons field jacket with OD wool shirt and trousers treated with anti-gas impregnation. On his right shoulder would be worn the gas detection brassard illustrated on B2 – this would change colour when exposed to chemical agents. The US Navy floatation belt he wears was also attached to important equipment so that if lost it would float ashore. If inflated by a heavily-loaded man who was out of his depth it was often lethal, tipping him upside down to drown. Besides his normal web equipment and the M1928 pack he carries the M5 assault gasmask in its black waterproof chest bag, and a general purpose ammunition bag. An Airborne-style aid pouch, including bandages, sulfa tablets, and two morphine syrettes ('one for pain, two for eternity'), is taped to his left shoulder brace – again, see B2; and he carries his M1 Garand in a clear Pliofilm cover. The helmet he is staring at reminds us that Rangers from the 2nd and 5th Bns landed on Dog Green and Dog White sectors of Omaha soon after the first waves of the 29th.

B2: 1st Lieutenant, 116th Infantry Regiment, 29th Infantry Division
The 29th was a National Guard division originating from Maryland, Virginia and Pennsylvania, and the blue and grey 'yin and yang' divisional sign symbolised unity created from the opposing Civil War histories of these states. It was among the first formations deployed to Britain, and stayed so long that it was nicknamed 'England's Own'; no doubt the division's personnel contributed honourably to the British stereotype of the GI as being 'over-sexed, over-paid and over here'.

The 29th landed on Omaha beach wearing fully painted helmets and with their chinstraps down. The men of both the 1st and 29th Divisions had their shoulder patch designs painted onto the fronts of their helmets for D-Day; 4th Division GIs commonly had them painted on their helmet liners. The divisional markings on helmets soon faded, and it became unusual to see them after the Normandy campaign.

This carbine-armed first lieutenant is uniformed essentially like his men, his rank marked by the bar painted on his helmet below the divisional sign, and metal insignia pinned to his epaulettes. Over the Parsons jacket he wears the assault vest, issued in quantity to D-Day units and not only to Rangers as is sometimes assumed. It was a rational approach to reform of the load-carrying web equipment, but was not much liked in practice – most were dumped soon after the landings, though not as swiftly as the M1926 US Navy lifebelts.

B3: T/5, Engineers, 2nd Infantry Division
Combat engineers played a key role in clearing water and beach obstacles on D-Day. Several types of joint Army/Navy engineer units were created for the invasion, and a number of volunteer engineers from the 2nd Division served with these. (The bulk of the 'Indianhead' division began to come ashore on D+1.) They wore anti-gas impregnated HBT fatigues over their woollen uniforms; some officers and many of the beach clearing personnel wore specially authorised paratroop boots. This engineer from the 2nd Division carries a purple smoke grenade – in case he has to signal landing troops to keep clear of an area rigged for demolition – and a demolition bag filled with half-pound or one-pound blocks of TNT. He sports a British-made aid pouch on his belt and would also be carrying an Airborne pouch. He is armed with a carbine, but like many GIs he may pick up the more powerful M1 Garand on the beach. The 2nd Division's most important action during the war was its stand holding the north shoulder of the 'Bulge' during the Ardennes fighting of December 1944. **(Inset)** 2nd Infantry Division patch.

C: OPERATION COBRA, NORMANDY, JULY 1944
C1: Rifleman, 41st Armored Infantry Regiment, 2nd Armored Division
Like the 3rd, the 2nd Armored was a 'heavy division' which had two tank regiments (66th and 67th Armor), each of three battalions, along with the three-battalion 41st Infantry. Its Combat Commands A & B landed over Omaha beach

Snatching a moment's rest during the savage fighting in the Normandy *bocage*, this battle-worn infantry sergeant from the 4th Division wears green HBT fatigues over his wool uniform (see Plate B3). He is armed with his M1, a spare bandoleer of ammunition and two 'frag' grenades. Like many GIs he seems to carry letters or photos from home stowed inside his helmet.

between 11 and 14 June, and it saw very heavy fighting during the July/August break-out from the beachhead areas. This lightly-equipped rifleman from the 41st Armored Infantry wears the so-called 'tanker jacket', which was actually commonly worn by many non-tank troops of armoured divisions, including the infantry. Otherwise his combat uniform and web equipment are standard. His gasmask has been 'lost', and his pack was last seen hanging off the side of his halftrack. Web canvas slings on M1 Garands began replacing the complex leather sling in mid-1944. It was common to see an 'immediate use' clip carried like this on a web brace or bandoleer sling, with the fabric trapped between the two rows of cartridges.

C2: BAR gunner, 8th Infantry Regiment, 4th Infantry Division

Every infantry squad had at least one man armed with the Browning Automatic Rifle. This 'Ivy' division GI carries a BAR with the bipod removed to save weight; he also has a Mk II fragmentation grenade. Like many GIs, he carries minimal equipment and has stuffed his 'M1941' field jacket into the back of his belt. The normal load carried by a BAR gunner was 13 x 20-round magazines – two in each pocket of the six-pocket belt, and one in the gun – but a designated assistant would carry two more belts. One 6ft 4in, 240lb BAR gunner from the 2nd Armored Division actually carried in combat 27 magazines in various pouches and pockets. Part of the 4th Division rode 2nd Armored Division tanks during 'Cobra'.

C3: Rifleman, 41st Armored Infantry Regiment, 2nd Armored Division

During the break-out the 2nd Armored Division swept through the initial oppositon, but on 28/29 July a fierce counter-attack by tanks and infantry from 2.SS-Panzer-Division 'Das Reich' hit the 2/41st Infantry and 3/67th Armor near St Denis-le-Gast. The attack was repulsed after desperate fighting, in the course of which LtCol Coleman, CO of the 2/41st, personally manned a bazooka before being killed in action. Later the division's Combat Command A served under the tactical command of the 29th Division.

While the great majority of infantry in Normandy wore the standard wool uniform, field jackets and/or herringbone twill fatigues, there was a limited experimental issue of the Army's two-piece M1942 camouflage uniform. Given the lush, sun-dappled terrain of summertime France this was reasonable. However, the resemblance of the unfamiliar printed pattern to that of the camouflage clothing routinely worn by the Waffen-SS troops encountered in Normandy led to its withdrawal after tragic cases of mistaken identity. Elements of the 2nd and 30th Infantry Divisions received this uniform, as did the 17th Engineer Bn and elements of the 41st Armored Infantry from the 2nd Armored Division; other individuals also received it when issued replacements for worn-out clothing during July and August. This figure is based on photographs of the 41st AIR taken by Robert Capa. The M1 helmet is garnished with a net and small strips of burlap scrim. Light field equipment is worn, without packs – like B1, this soldier travels in a halftrack and stows his gear on the vehicle. His web belt carries 80 rounds and the expendable bandoleer has an additional 48 rounds.

D: FRANCE, 1944

D1: Corporal, Women's Army Corps; Supreme Headquarters Allied Expeditionary Forces, Versailles

This WAC corporal is serving at SHAEF as a member of the Signal Corps, thereby 'freeing a man to fight'. By the end of the war 140,000 WACs were serving in the US Army. She wears the new WAC curved-cut overseas cap piped with the old gold and light green branch colours; these were in short supply, and many WACs wore the men's overseas cap without piping. The tailored female service dress uniform with plastic buttons bears US and Signal Corps collar discs, though the WAC's own Athena-head emblem was often worn. She wears ribbons for the ETO and the WAC Medal marking service in the pre-1943 WAAC. By the end of the year WACs in the ETO could expect to receive the short WAC 'Ike' jacket. Her laced russet brown shoes were known as the 'gruesome twosome' due to their appearance and fit. She carries an issue shoulder bag ('purse').

(Inset) This tab in WAAC colours was ordered worn on the sleeves, below any rank chevrons, from 25 March 1942.

Operation Cobra, July 1944: two GIs from the 41st Armored Infantry, 2nd Armored Division watch over a seriously wounded buddy during the Normandy break-out battles. All wear the two-piece camouflage fatigues briefly issued to some units in Normandy (see Plate C3). The casualty has been treated and tagged by the medics. The Thompson gunner, probably a squad leader, also carries a fragmentation and a smoke grenade. (Photo Robert Capa, Magnum)

During the Battle of the Bulge a chaplain (second right, wearing an Air Corps flight jacket) stops to chat to men of the 2nd Bn/504th PIR, 82nd Airborne Division. Most of the paratroopers wear wool overcoats or raincoats (see Plate F2); some carry 'hobo' bedrolls slung with rope instead of packs.

It was discontinued in July 1943 when the WAAC was transformed into the WAC – from Auxiliaries into full members of the US armed forces.

D2: Sergeant, 104th Infantry Regiment, 26th Infantry Division

This NCO from the New England National Guard 26th 'YD' or 'Yankee Division', taking a coffee break, wears M1943 HBT fatigues over his wool uniform. Promotion came quickly in combat, and his rank has been hastily inked onto his sleeves. He is armed with an M1 (side-bolt) Thompson SMG, and carries smoke and fragmentation grenades. His small haversack-style bag is a limited issue item for holding 30-round Thompson magazines. This sergeant's wire-framed glasses are standard GI issue. The 'YD' division first saw action around Metz in November 1944, where it worked closely with the 761st Tank Battalion.

D3: Captain, 761st Tank Battalion (Colored); Metz, November 1944

By VE-Day the Army had two Tank (761st & 784th) and two Tank Destroyer (614th & 827th) battalions of black GIs. When they joined his 3rd Army the essentially racist Gen George S. Patton told the 761st, 'I don't care what colour you are as long as you go up there and kill those Kraut sons-of-bitches'. For its record in World War II this crack battalion would receive a long-delayed Distinguished Unit Citation only in 1978. The 761st worked comfortably with the 26th Infantry and 17th Airborne divisions, but did not fare as well when serving with other divisions of a more Southern origin.

African-American GIs wore all the standard uniforms and insignia of the US Army. This captain wears the tanker's jacket (some officers had theirs modified by adding epaulettes), and the bib-fronted cold weather overtrousers. His rank is shown on his helmet, and pinned through leather patches to the jacket shoulders. The M1 was worn along with the armoured crew helmet by tank personnel – and sometimes even on top of it. Like many tankers, this officer sports a .45 pistol in an M7 shoulder holster.

E: NETHERLANDS, OCTOBER 1944

E1: Major, 23rd Armored Infantry Regiment, 7th Armored Division

The 7th Armored Division fought a month-long series of tank battles near Overloon/Venlo in the Netherlands in October

1944. The division's most important action would come two months later, with its CCB's defence of and break-out from St Vith in the Ardennes. This major's rank is only just visible on his shirt collar; veteran officers and NCOs commonly kept the wearing of insignia to a minimum to increase their life-span. As a major he is probably the CO or second-in-command (executive officer, 'XO') of his battalion, and here he is talking over the SCR 300 radio with one of his companies; the scale of issue was six SCR 300s per battalion – two of these FM sets for Bn HQ and one each for the company headquarters. The batteries in the lower component of the backpack gave about 24 hours' use. The officer wears, as an alternative to the field or tanker's jackets, the third-pattern US Army mackinaw in cotton poplin with a notched, unfaced collar and without the integral cloth belt of earlier models. Herringbone twill trousers are tucked into a pair of the much sought-after paratrooper boots. He is armed with a .45 pistol and a M1 carbine with 15-round magazines; the pistol is carried in a custom-modified open-top M1916 holster.

E2: Private first class, radio operator, 23rd Armored Infantry Regiment, 7th Armored Division

Neither the woollen 'ETO jacket' nor its smarter cousin, the M1944 'Ike jacket', were commonly seen worn by front-line GIs, but it was not unknown. This Pfc has sewn his prewar silver-on-black rank stripes on the sleeves of his short British-made ETO jacket. Though 'buckle boots' were coming into issue in the autumn of 1944 this GI still wears the old 'service shoes' and canvas leggings. Sufficiently weighed down by his 34lb SCR 300 radio, he is otherwise very lightly equipped. The belt that came as part of the radio's rig would not accept any other equipment items, so he wears a pistol belt for his canteen, aid pouch and the magazine pouch for the carbine, which is his regulation weapon. The axe-shaped canvas bag looped to the radio belt is the BG150, which held the radio handset and both long and short sectional antennae. Within the infantry company the platoons communicated with the 'handie-talkie' SCR 536 AM radio.

E3: Captain, Forward Air Controller, US 9th Army Air Force

Close co-operation between ground troops and the tactical aircraft which more or less ruled the skies over the ETO in

1944-45 was a major factor in the successful Allied advance. Pilots were assigned for limited periods of service with front-line units, to provide a knowledgeable link between them and the supporting Air Corps. Unfortunately, US planes sometimes hit friendly units during the battles for France, prompting the infantry – particularly the unfortunate 30th Division, who were bombed several times between Normandy and the Bulge – to rename the 9th Air Force the '9th Luftwaffe'. This air controller wears his rank and 9th AAF shoulder patch on a trenchcoat of a darkish green shade, a version commonly worn in England and sometimes by front-line officers. He too is fortunate in having obtained a pair of 'Corcorans'. Hidden here, a .45 pistol is holstered on his right hip. Nearby, no doubt, is a radio vehicle capable of direct communications with circling P-47 fighter-bombers.

F: BASTOGNE, DECEMBER 1944
F1: Rifleman, 28th Infantry Division
The 28th Division was originally a National Guard outfit from Pennsylvania, the 'Keystone State'. Its red keystone patch was nicknamed by the 28th's GIs the 'Bloody Bucket' after its losses in Normandy and – with the 4th and 8th Divisions – in the meatgrinder of the Hürtgen Forest; the 28th was then sent to the 'quiet' Ardennes sector to rest... Its two-day stand in the face of the advancing 5.Panzer-Armee gave the 101st Airborne time to occupy Bastogne. This soldier, wearing a 'home-ripped' snow camouflage cape and helmet cover made from a bedsheet, is probably from the Quartermaster company or some other divisional support unit, pitched into the fighting at short notice. Under his sheet he wears a first-pattern mackinaw with wool-faced shawl collar, a five-button sweater, the usual drab wool trousers, a pair of the new M1943 'buckle boots', and wool trigger-finger gloves. His equipment is minimal: a rifle belt, and a musette to carry all his other gear.

F2: Bazooka gunner, 327th Glider Infantry Regiment, 101st Airborne Division
The standard issue enlisted men's wool melton overcoat was much used by the Airborne during the Battle of the Bulge.

(One paratrooper of the 82nd is reputed to have said to a worried tank crew, 'Looking for a safe place? Well, buddy, just pull in behind me.') Under his coat this 'glider-rider' wears the standard M1943 combat jacket and buckle boots now becoming common throughout the ETO. His baggy trousers with cargo pockets are the only remaining sure sign of his Airborne status, though his belt equipment includes one of the limited-issue 'rigger's' ammunition pouches peculiar to the Airborne. He is armed with the M1 carbine, and a M3 trench knife strapped to his boot; some photos show civilian knives carried as well. His main weapon, however, is the latest M9 folding version of the 2.36in anti-tank rocket launcher or 'bazooka'. A white 'club' helmet symbol identifies his regiment.

(Inset) By 1945 the 'glider-riders' finally received this 'wings' badge and the same hazardous duty pay as their parachute brethren. The bronze stars mark two combat landings, in Normandy and Holland.

F3: T/5, 20th Armored Infantry Regiment, 10th Armored Division
Active in the capture of Metz in November 1944, the 10th Armored Division had its Combat Command B inside Bastogne throughout the siege. This GI wears the new four-pocket, sateen-shell M1943 field jacket, introduced as a universal garment for all branches of service; he has not yet received the matching trousers, but is fortunate in having secured himself a pair of M1944 shoepacs. He is armed with the M1 Garand, and grenades including a smooth-cased Mk III concussion type. Among his belt equipment is the folding-head entrenching tool based on a German design, with a cut-down haft. His web equipment is in the new greener OD shade 7 now reaching the front in quantity, although existing stocks of items in the sandier shade 9 would continue to be issued for years. Since it is of little practical use this GI has dispensed with his bayonet. More useful is the blanket just visible tucked through the back of his belt. He is carrying the baseplate for an 81mm mortar.

Along with the 101st Airborne and 10th Armored the Bastogne garrison included elements of the 9th Armored

Operation Market Garden, September 1944: a classic shot of an 82nd Airborne Division lieutenant and NCOs going over the orders before putting on their 'chutes for the drop over Holland. With the issue of the well-liked M1943 field jacket after D-Day the special M1942 paratrooper's jacket began to be a rarity. The buckle boots also began to replace the jump boots in the Airborne, much to the annoyance of paratroopers. Note (left) the white-painted horizontal NCOs' recognition stripe on the back of the corporal's helmet.

and 28th Infantry divisions, the 705th Tank Destroyer Bn, 1128th Engineer Combat Group, and five corps-level artillery battalions.

G: GERMANY, SPRING 1945
G1: 2nd Lieutenant, Army Nurse Corps
Some 60,000 nurses served in the Army during World War II, and many went into harm's way; for instance, about 200 served in the Anzio beachhead, where six were killed in action and four won the Silver Star. Nurses were fully commissioned in 1943 with the majority ranked as second lieutenants. This nurse wears the WAC issue two-piece herringbone twill fatigues, quickly identifiable by the slanted thigh pockets and the reversed buttoning. She displays her rank painted on her helmet and pinned to her right collar, balanced by the caduceus with superimposed 'N' of the ANC; like all medical personnel she is entitled to wear the red cross brassard. She carries a musette bag pressed into service as a medical haversack and roughly marked as such. US Army nurses played their part in the ghastly task faced by the Allied troops who unexpectedly found themselves liberating Nazi concentration camps as they rolled across Germany in 1945.

G2: Rifleman, 89th Infantry Division
The 'Rolling W' division was one of the first across the Rhine; as it raced into Germany its advancing columns were led by captured Wehrmacht vehicles hastily overpainted with white stars, and two German fire engines with sirens blaring. As part of 3rd Army the 4th Armored and 89th Divisions found the first concentration camp liberated by the Western Allies – Ohrdruf, near Gotha, on 4 April. This typical infantryman of the last weeks of the war – here shown handling an M1942 litter – wears the new two-part M1944 'combat and cargo' pack standardised in July 1944 as the replacement for the old M1928. The lower, cargo bag for non-essentials could be unfastened easily from the upper, combat section holding the immediate necessities; the blanket roll and entrenching tool were attached to the upper bag. Another new item is the

bag for the lightweight gasmask, worn on the left hip; the gasmask itself may have been dumped, however, as the bag made a handy repository for personal kit. Note finally that an elasticated band was now being issued for the small mesh helmet net.

G3: Private first class, medical orderly, 45th Infantry Division
The 45th 'Thunderbird', along with elements of several other divisions including the 42nd 'Rainbow', liberated Dachau concentration camp and its satellites on 29 April 1945. This medic's left arm shows his divisional patch, rank and red cross brassard; the latter was individually numbered and registered to the wearer, as the status of those claiming the protection of the Geneva Convention was a serious matter (medics also carried annotated ID cards – 'Geneva cards'). Photos show a number of different styles of red cross markings used in the ETO; at Dachau medics of the 45th were photographed with this four-circle presentation under wide mesh nets. His pair of medical bags are carried on a special yoke harness with a very broad rear shoulder piece; the basic load in these included dressings and bandages of various types, iodine swabs, ointments for burn and eye treatments, a tourniquet, morphine syrettes, and a duplicate pad of labels for describing treatment given and attachment to the casualty. Besides a medic's ability to slow blood loss, his administering of morphine was perhaps the most important thing he could do to prevent a wounded man from going into potentially fatal shock. His nickname among front-line GIs was invariably 'Doc'. Other than knives, medics in the ETO went unarmed; they routinely carried two canteens on their belts. **(Inset)** Being non-combatants, front-line medics were not allowed the Combat Infantryman's Badge. After much lobbying, they were authorised the Combat Medic Badge in early 1945.

H: ARMY OF OCCUPATION, 1945
Three veterans celebrate victory, out on the town in their spiffiest uniforms, displaying all the badges and decorations which they have richly earned. Note that one of them is still of an age which might make it hard for him to buy a beer in some states of the USA without showing identification.
H1: Warrant Officer glider pilot, 61st Troop Carrier Group, US 9th Army Air Force
As was common among flying officers, his cap and jacket are of officers' quality and, apart from his specific rank bar in gilt and brown enamel on the epaulettes, he wears officers' style badges. This aviator has a '50 mission crush' service cap, an officers' M1944 OD wool field jacket ('Ike' jacket) and matching trousers in a dark 'chocolate' shade, and an officers' chocolate shirt set off with a pale necktie. On his left chest the silver glider pilot's wings are distinguished by a 'G' – they used to say this stood for 'Guts'. Below are a typical

Part of a group photo of command and staff personnel from the 17th Airborne Division chuted up ready for Operation Varsity, the joint US/British drop across the Rhine in March 1945; after serving in the Ardennes this was the 17th's only airborne deployment. All wear the M1943 field jacket apart from (standing second left) one with the M1943 jacket's pile liner, and (kneeling right) the lieutenant in the old M1942 Airborne field uniform, as illustrated in MAA 347.

Germany, early 1945: officers of the 5th Ranger Bn still wearing their D-Day 'Sunoco' diamond-shaped Ranger shoulder patches, and probably also the orange Ranger diamond on the backs of their helmets. They wear 'tanker jackets' and matching trousers (left), an Air Corps flight jacket (second right) and a mackinaw. Among the visible weapons are a bazooka, a .30cal machine gun, two M1 rifles, an M3 'grease gun' and a Thompson, taped grenades and a captured P08 Luger.

array of ribbons; *NB on most of these plates these naturally reproduce too small for identification, but representative selections are listed – here,* the Bronze Star, Air Medal (with two oakleaf clusters marking three awards), Purple Heart, American Service, and ETO Medal with an invasion arrowhead and two campaign stars; on the right chest is the blue Distinguished Unit Citation (DUC). His four overseas service bars mark two years abroad. Late in the war glider pilots added Airborne tabs to their Air Force patches on the left shoulder. His polaroid aviator sunglasses became very popular among GIs.

While not illustrated here, in 1945 combat officers in command positions were authorised green 'leadership tabs' to be worn looped over their epaulettes.

H2: T/5, 505th Parachute Infantry Regiment, 82nd Airborne Division

This paratrooper wears the overseas cap and an enlisted man's 'Ike' jacket, with the earlier drab wool trousers common throughout the war bloused into spit-shined jump boots. The cap bears the 505th PIR enamelled metal crest at right front, because the left is occupied by the combined parachute/glider patch of the Airborne. His rank is marked by the new issue green-on-black stripes. Having served 18 months' overseas in the infantry, he has transferred into the Signal Corps – a fact shown only by the crossed flags on his left collar disc. On the lower collars are enamelled versions of the divisional patch of the 82nd Airborne as worn on his left shoulder; the right shoulder patch denotes his combat service under the 1st Allied Airborne Army. He wears parachute wings on the regimentally coloured backing of the 505th, the Combat Infantryman's Badge and the DUC. His ribbons are for the Bronze Star, Purple Heart, Good Conduct Medal, ETO Medal with arrowhead and three stars, and American Campaign Medal. The lanyards – *fourragères* – mark collective awards to his unit by the Allied nations which the 82nd helped to liberate: on his right shoulder the Belgian Croix de Guerre, on his left the French Croix de Guerre and

the orange cord of Holland's Wilhelm Order. His expert marksmanship badge sports three 'shingles' for rifle, bayonet and grenade.

(Inset right) Parachutist's qualification wings, on the blue and red oval backing adopted by the 505th PIR. Stars or arrowheads were sometimes fixed to the badge to represent combat jumps.

H3: 1st Sergeant, 26th Infantry Regiment, 1st Infantry Division

This long service first sergeant in his late 30s wears the overseas cap, 'Ike' jacket and trousers in slightly differing shades of OD, and a pair of 'buckle boots', which he has painstakingly shaved and waxed to a shine. (In 1947 the Army were obliged to convert their footwear to universal Department of Defense black; World War II veterans would boast of having served in the old 'brown shoe Army'.) His cap is piped infantry light blue and bears the 26th Infantry's enamelled crest. His rank is shown by early-style silver-on-black chevrons and rockers. The shoulder patch of the 'Big Red One' marks one of the most battle-experienced formations in the ETO, and his left chest identifies a soldier highly decorated for valour in combat. Beneath the CIB, here a version in silver embroidery on blue, might be seen the ribbons for the Silver Star and Bronze Star (with oakleaf clusters marking repeat awards); the Purple Heart (also with clusters); the Good Conduct Medal with one 'tie'; the American Campaign Medal; and the ETO Medal with the arrowhead marking participation in at least one amphibious (or airborne) invasion, and one silver and three bronze stars for eight distinct campaigns. He too will soon be authorised the French and Belgian Croix de Guerre lanyards. This 'top sergeant' also sports the marksman's badge with two 'shingles'.

(Inset left) The 'Ruptured Duck'. Ex-servicemen were allowed to wear their uniforms for 60 days after mustering out, but had to sew this patch over the right pocket of their uniform tunic to show their status.

BIBLIOGRAPHY

Adleman, R. & Walton, G. *The Champagne Campaign*, 1969

Ambrose, S. Citizen Soldiers, 1997

Andrews, J. *Airborne Album*, Vol I, 1982

Bergerud, E. *Touched with Fire*, 1996

Canfield, B. *US Infantry Weapons of World War II*, 1994

Ellis, J. World War II: *The Sharp End*, 1990; US title *On the Front Lines*, 1991

Ellis, J. *The World War II Date Book*, 1993

Forty, G. *US Army Handbook 1939-45*, 1995

Gawne, J. *The War in the Pacific*, 1996

Gawne, J. *Spearheading D-Day*, 1998

Katcher, P. *US 2nd Armored Division 1940-45* (Osprey Vanguard 11), 1979

Ladd, J. *Commandos and Rangers of World War II*, 1978

Langellier, J. *The War in Europe*, 1995

Lewis, K. *Doughboy to GI: US Army Clothing and Equipment 1900-1945*, 1993

Maguire, J. *Silver Wings, Pinks & Greens*, 1994

Mansoor, P. *The GI Offensive in Europe*, 1999

Mauldin, W. *Upfront*, 1944

Mayo, L. *The Ordnance Department: Beachhead to Battlefront*, 1996

McManus, J. *The Deadly Brotherhood*, 1998

Rentz, B. *Geronimo*, 1998

Rottman, G. & Volstad, R. *US Army Airborne 1940-90* (Osprey Elite 31), 1990

Rottman, G. & Volstad, R. *US Army Rangers 1942-87* (Osprey Elite 13), 1987

Rottman, G. & Volstad, R. *US Army Combat Equipments 1910-1988* (Osprey MAA 205), 1989

Schreier, K. *Tanks & Artillery*, 1994

Stanton, S. *US Army Uniforms of World War II*, 1991

Sylvia, S. & O'Donnell, M. *Uniforms, Weapons and Equipment of the World War II GI*, 1982

Windrow, R. & Hawkins, T. *The World War II GI: US Army Uniforms 1941-45 in Color Photographs*, 1993

Zaloga, S. *Armour of the Pacific War* (Osprey Vanguard 35), 1983

Zaloga, S. *Sherman Medium Tank 1941-45* (Osprey New Vanguard 3), 1993

Zaloga, S. *Amtracs – US Amphibious Assault Vehicles* (Osprey New Vanguard 30), 1999

Zaloga, S. *M3 & M5 Stuart Light Tanks 1940-45* (Osprey New Vanguard 33), 1999

INDEX